POLITICALLY DEFINED

Memoir of an Unknown Activist

Dinah Yessne

GOODRICH MEMORIAL LIBRARY
202 MAIN STREET
NEWPORT, VT 05855
(802) 334-7902

Politically Defined: Memoir of an Unknown Activist
Dinah Yessne

Copyright © 2020 Dinah Yessne

All rights reserved. No part of this book may be reproduced in any form without permission in writing from the author, except by a reviewer, who may quote brief passages.

ISBN: 978-0-578-79230-9

Library of Congress Control Number: 2020920637

Interior design by Gareth Bentall
Politics and Prose Bookstore
Washington, D.C.

Cover design by Sally Stetson
Sally Stetson Design
Stowe, Vermont

Printed in the United States of America

www.politicallydefined.com

GOODRICH MEMORIAL LIBRARY
202 MAIN STREET
NEWPORT, VT 05855
(802) 334-7902

Dedicated to the Memory of
Justice Ruth Bader Ginsburg

1933 - 2020

CONTENTS

POLITICALLY DEFINED

DEFINED

Memoir of an Unknown Activist

Introduction

One evening in the early summer of 1988, the phone rang at my home in St. Johnsbury, Vermont. The woman on the other end of the line identified herself as Madeleine Kunin, then the governor of Vermont. The governor has a distinctive voice and there was no question about her authenticity. I suppose I made some pleasant remark after she introduced herself, but really, I don't remember. I was startled to have the governor on the other end of my phone and couldn't imagine what she was calling me about.

She quickly got down to the reason for her call. "Dinah, I'm calling to ask you to run for the legislature from St. Johnsbury in the upcoming November election." Running for the legislature from St. Johnsbury was something no Democrat had bothered to do since 1980, the year I had moved to town with my family. St. Johnsbury was considered such a bastion of conservatism that Republican candidates had simply run unopposed for the past eight years, a fact the governor and I both knew well.

I had built a strong reputation in the community by then. A member of the St. Johnsbury Democratic Committee since 1983, I was serving as its chair and had been elected a justice of the peace and member of the Board of Civil Authority. I had also chaired Caledonia County's Equal Rights Amendment campaign, and following Vermont's defeat of the Amendment had kept the dream of local women alive by co-founding the Caledonia County Women's Network. But let's face it, I was easily identified as a progressive Democrat. My chance of being elected to the legislature from St. Johnsbury was next to nonexistent.

"But Dinah," the governor said in answer to my demur, "we can't just hand it to them on a silver platter."

My feeling was that if the governor asks you to do something, you ought to do it, if you possibly can. But my interest in what she had to say went deeper than that. I've always had an underlying belief that in a democratic society everyone has an obligation to serve in some way. The question is, what form should it take? The governor's simply stated reason for running resonated with me. Standing there with the phone in my hand and the governor on the other end, running for the state legislature seemed a reasonable thing to do.

The practical issues were considerable. I had a solo law practice at the time that I was barely managing as it was. My husband, Jim Keeney, was then the director of Northeast Kingdom Community Action (NEKCA), a federally funded community action agency with a tri-county catchment area that covered 2,013 square miles in the northeastern corner of the state. He was already commuting forty-three miles one way to work in Newport on a daily basis, and I knew enough about political campaigns and my own intense approach to any new endeavor to know that much of the care and feeding of our two children, Elizabeth, 7, and Daniel, 4, would fall to him if I ran.

And what *of* the children? How would they fit into this? These were questions that had to be answered together, but I knew that as he had done throughout our marriage whenever I'd asked for his support, Jim would give it immediately, and without reservation. Somehow we would figure it out.

I announced my candidacy on July 12 on page one of the *Caledonian-Record,* our local newspaper. The *Record*, which had never been my friend, had nonetheless always been more than fair about printing my press releases verbatim. They did not let me down on either count at any time over the next four months, printing whatever I gave them, but endorsing my opponents.

My platform was the quality of representation I would provide generally, and my strong interest in improving the economic life of St. Johnsbury's working families and struggling small business owners. In addition, by responding to the governor's request, I was giving people a choice when they went to the polls.

I didn't assemble an advisory committee to help me decide whether to run. The wisdom of running was never really on the table; it seemed a sure thing I was going to lose. Nonetheless, I spent the next four months knocking on virtually every door in St. Johnsbury, getting to know streets and neighborhoods I'd previously barely noticed, gaining some new impressions of the town, and having some decidedly nonpolitical experiences.

In a speech I made to the Caledonia County Women's Network during the campaign, which I tried to keep nonpartisan, I highlighted some of those experiences: my first dog attack on Concord Avenue and first dog bite on Spring Street; the hospitality of delinquent tax collector Ron Wilkie, who invited me in to see his wonderful collection of old mustache cups; actually noticing for the first time the cliff after which Cliff Street was named; and the depressing words of the elementary school teacher who told me she didn't have time to register to vote or go to the polls.

Most thought provoking was seeing all the different sizes, shapes, and conditions of the houses in the town, and realizing how different the lives being lived inside them were, as well as hearing the different values and concerns of the people I met, and really coming to understand the challenge it would be to represent the diverse residents of an entire town.

The campaign turned out to be a good experience for the entire family. I remember with a smile the evening we all spent marching around our round dining room table feeling useful and important as we systematically put packets of literature together for a mailing. The kids often went door to door with me, Daniel in his stroller and Elizabeth pushing him. There were campaign events that we could all attend together, and which we all enjoyed. When there were events I couldn't take the kids to and Jim was busy, I used campaign funds to pay for child care. I had requested and received an opinion from the Vermont secretary of state that campaign contributions could be expended for child care expenses when necessary to campaign. This opinion was confirmed in 2018 by the Federal Elections Commission, when so many women came forward to run for political office.

Friends, acquaintances, and people I'd never met came out of the woodwork with excitement over a chance to express themselves politically again. Community leaders agreed to endorse me in newspaper ads and radio spots. Others hosted house parties and fundraisers around town and beyond, lending their names and financial backing for a half-page endorsement in the newspaper. To say it was gratifying doesn't do justice to how I felt about the support I received from so many people. The *Caledonian-Record* described the campaign as "what some are calling one of the most exciting House races in the county."[1]

Regrettably, there wasn't much opportunity to speak to the issues. Candidate forums were few and far between; I remember only two. Door-to-door conversations were frequent, but most people are uncomfortable talking politics with a stranger, and were content to greet me, take my measure, and accept a brochure to read after I left.

---

[1] The *Caledonian-Record,* November 7, 1988, 1.

Election Day fell on my birthday. We wanted to run a radio ad that would remind my supporters to vote, yet wouldn't offend by being too pushy. We went with something light and cute: Elizabeth introducing herself and saying simply, "Vote for my mom, it's her birthday today!" As we gathered that night to await the results, I pondered how I'd gotten to this point in the first place, and what could possibly come next.

Chapter One
Small But Mighty
1945

I was born nine weeks ahead of schedule on November 8, 1945, weighed in at three pounds twelve-and-a-half ounces, and was only sixteen-and-a-half inches long. In this high-tech day and age no one would blink an eye about it, but back then it was a big deal. As a result of my physical deficits I spent the first five weeks of my life in a plexiglas box at St. Paul's Midway Hospital in plain view of anyone who wanted a look. This was my introduction to public life.

The result of this lifelong predicament of being premature and small has had a considerable effect on me that should not be underestimated. As a child what were common successes and failures for my friends—such as trying to steal second base in a baseball game, for instance—for me became major incidents worthy of remark, typically, "You always were in a hurry!" I was always the shortest in my class with the exception of one year when Sara-Jane Ramras slipped behind; but she could speak German so it didn't affect her status.

Things even reached a point where I once asked my mother, then a social worker helping World War II refugees prepare affidavits for reparation, to notarize a statement for me attesting to my true age. This, I hoped, would quiet my tormentors, who insisted I was too small to be the age I said I was.

Most significantly, shortly before she died, my mother said to me with foreboding, "Remember—you're not as strong as you think you are." I have worried about this warning for well over fifty years, and will no doubt worry about it until the day I do actually die. The lifetime of anxiety regarding susceptibility to this and predisposition to that, which her comment engendered, has taken its toll over the years.

At one point I received a gift that softened a bit the blow of my size. I was attending the lab school at the University of Minnesota in Minneapolis, University Elementary School, or UES as we called it. This made me and my classmates handy guinea pigs for a variety of experiments conducted by researchers from the various U of M departments and graduate schools.

The gift resulted from a study of fat. Those of us who had been selected for the study were escorted to one of the medical school buildings, where we changed into bathing suits of known weight. One by one we were strapped into a leather sling and swung out over a large tub of water, then gently lowered into the tub to see how much water we displaced.

It was very exciting and much more fun than being asked, as we were on other occasions, to eat chocolate-covered ants and grasshoppers, or to make designs out of brightly colored wooden blocks. But the best part of the study for me, by far, was having my bones measured before immersion. I was told that were my legs in perfect proportion to my torso, I would be 5'6" when fully grown! For someone who never topped 5'1" before starting to go in the other direction, this was heady stuff and has always made me feel close to normal when sitting down at a table with others, where the length of my legs is unimportant.

Despite my size, once I emerged from the plexiglas box I became something of a wild child, in perpetual motion, if family stories are to be believed. Asked to describe my favorite activities at age three in my Better

Homes & Gardens baby book, my mother listed "climbing furniture" and "racing through the halls."

It was not unusual for my parents to lose all track of me around this time. This may have been because I had an older brother, Peter, and it was easy for them to assume that I was with him, which indeed was often the case. Or, it may have been because my parents had built one of the first modern homes in Highland Park, a neighborhood in St. Paul. Although it was a small ranch with a typical floor plan, they spent what extra money they had on custom interior features, including many compartments into which my brother and I were forever placing ourselves and each other so we could disappear.

And in truth, parents just didn't worry about where their kids were in those days anywhere near as much as they do today. For my mother, who was hospitalized with a nervous breakdown after a miscarriage between my brother's birth and my own three years later, and who was plagued by depression at various points in her life, I suspect it was something of a relief when we both disappeared at the same time.

Family friends and relatives have their favorite stories about my activities during this period; but to my mind the most significant one was the hitchhiking episode. Having free time to play, Peter and I had opted for the woods. At that time the woods ran thickly for a couple of city blocks between the street our house was on, Mt. Curve Boulevard, and what we called the River Road, a curving scenic drive along the Mississippi River.

In 1948 the woods were dense and undeveloped. The area served as a jungle playground for us kids, who spent a great deal of time there feeding rabbits, building brush forts, and ambushing each other. Every now and then we lost track of each other and our bearings, and on this particular day, when I found myself alone all the way on the other side of the woods at the River Road, I decided to find out why it was that some people stood in the street with one foot on the curb and their thumb in the air. I struck the characteristic pose of a hitchhiker and a car stopped almost immediately. An incredulous woman asked me kindly and gently what I was doing.

"I don't know," I answered matter of factly.

"Are you hitchhiking?" she inquired. That question was a bit more difficult to answer since hitchhiking wasn't something I had any knowledge about.

"Well, if you are hitchhiking, get in," she said, which I did. "Now," she continued, "where do you live?" I gave my address as I had been taught and was quickly delivered back home to my amazed parents, who as usual had not yet realized I was missing.

The hitchhiking story has been told and retold, the focus always on my cuteness, my precociousness, and the very great luck of it all. But working it out in my mind years later I realized that the sense of not-quite-rightness that often came over me each time the tale was told was based on the possibility that I might have been in real danger, and that this was not just one such time, but only the first I remembered.

My early fearlessness, born out of the freedom I was given as a young child, no doubt played a significant part in what later became a bold willingness to take on the dangers of public life. Years later K. C. Whiteley, an astute and no-nonsense commentator on the state of the world generally, wrote a letter of recommendation for me that explained the number and variety of my activities on behalf of women and other underrepresented groups by saying, "Dinah is essentially fearless."

I had certainly never thought of myself as fearless, and I know for certain that I am not. But the fact that she thought so gave me pause, and I realized that in the realm she was addressing, she was right. My childhood, however difficult it may have been for my parents to get me through it, did instill in me a nature that was not afraid of much. Not afraid to take risks, question authority, or take on challenging situations. This, I believe, together with the social values my parents transmitted to me by example about how and for whom one's life should be lived, led directly to my long involvement in politics and to a life, overall, that has been politically defined.

My great-grandparents, M.D. and Masha Mirviss, with their six children and a sampling of grandchildren. My mother, Evelyn Mirviss Yessne is third from the left; my father, Howard Yessne, is at the far left.

Chapter Two

Nature Meets Nurture

1948

I f fearlessness was my nature, the social values I acquired came from long family traditions of hard work and a commitment to making things better for others.

My father was Howard Yessne. His family on both sides had come to the United States from Eastern Europe, around the turn of the century. They were part of a mass migration of Jews from lands ruled by Russia, fleeing a wave of state-sponsored massacres known as *pogroms,* which capped centuries of ill-treatment under the czars.

My father's maternal grandparents were Bernard and Sadie Shapiro. They migrated from Russia in 1885 and settled in St. Paul, where Bernard took up his trade as a shoemaker again, and Sue, my grandmother and the third of their five children, was the first to be born in the United States. My father's paternal grandparents came from Pereyaslav, Ukraine. My grandfather Herman was the son of William Yessne and Sarah Bulkin, who settled in Duluth, Minnesota in 1905, then moved to St. Paul when my father and his sister were in high school. Herman's grandparents had been tailor and dressmaker to Russian aristocracy, and as an adult he adopted their trade and started the Grand Garment Manufacturing Company in downtown St. Paul's warehouse district, making outerwear for children and adults.

When the Great Depression hit, my father was called upon to leave his engineering studies at the University of Minnesota to help in his father's factory. He never returned to college, and when his father died, he took over the business and ran it himself. Not having a head for business, however, he couldn't keep it going. He was as hard a worker as I've ever known, toiling six days a week for forty years in the only business he knew, and by sheer determination providing our family with a middle-class lifestyle by going in and out of various garment manufacturing companies as an owner or partner here, or a manager there, but never making a lasting success of running his own business.

As a child I was only vaguely aware of my father's occupational challenges, knowing that there were some years when my mother went to work outside our home and others when she didn't, and that the place where my father worked changed from time to time. But I learned about hard work from his example, and changing work sites periodically seemed a normal thing to do.

Everyone who knew my father liked him and admired his sense of humor. In keeping with his warm, compassionate nature he had very loyal employees, most memorably George Radke, an experienced fabric cutter, and Catherine Kordosky, an accomplished seamstress who was his forewoman. As a child I sometimes went to work with him on a Saturday morning, or when I was a bit older, met him for lunch after roaming around downtown. I got to know the rhythm of the factories on those extra days when George, Catherine, and my father were there catching up on orders that needed to go out. I can still picture him walking swiftly around one factory or another with a worried look on his face and some apparently important little slip of paper in his hand, no doubt looking for a bundle of fabric pieces of a particular size and color. He remained in the garment industry until Alzheimer's Disease robbed him of the ability to keep details straight. When he eventually came to live with me and my family in Vermont, two of his most repetitive gestures were walking around clutching little pieces of paper, and rubbing his thumb and forefinger together as if appreciating the feel of cloth. It seemed that this was all he could remember from his many years of hard work.

Unlike my father, my mother, Evelyn Mirviss, came from a large family, and a very close one, and my brother and I knew them all growing up, even though many of her relatives, including four sets of her aunts and uncles, had migrated from the Twin Cities to the West Coast before we were born and established their families there. Out of the four sets of aunts and uncles three were heavily involved in progressive or left-wing political causes.[2] Family vacations in both directions, and milestone events, kept us in touch with all of them.

My mother's parents, Jean Rosenbloom and Jacob (Jack) Mirviss, were first cousins who came from a long line of respected rabbis, cantors,

---

[2] Uncle Michael Loring, born Samuel Mirviss, was part of the New York activist community in the 1930s and a friend of Woody Guthrie, Pete Seeger, Paul Robeson and Theodore Bikel, among others. He travelled with Henry Wallace and wrote campaign songs for him with Seeger, and was the first to introduce the song "Joe Hill" to the labor and activist communities. He returned from WWII with a bronze star, and settled in Fresno, California, where he began a distinguished thirty-four year career as a cantor rather than return to show business. Refusing to name names during the Red Scare, he remained active in civil rights and antiwar efforts, along with his wife June, an early and lifelong member of the Women's International League for Peace and Freedom. "Michael Loring: A Portland Folk Music Connection," Portland Folkmusic Society, *Local Lore* 42:2, 5-6. Uncle Phil Shapiro, married to Sophia Mirviss, was a prominent San Francisco psychiatrist and psychoanalyst considered "physician to the movement." He helped found Physicians for Social Responsibility in 1962 and chaired the San Francisco Medical Community for Human Rights during the Vietnam War era. A longtime peace activist, his work focused on disarmament. Phillip Shapiro obituary, *San Francisco Chronicle*, December 30, 1985. Uncle Reuben Lenske, married to Rose Mirviss, was a leftwing civil rights lawyer in Portland, Oregon, who was disbarred in 1964 after a conviction for alleged tax fraud. Two years later the conviction was reversed on appeal by the Ninth Circuit Court of Appeals, which found the case "nothing less than a witch-hunt, a crusade...to rid our society of unorthodox thinkers and actors by using federal income tax laws and federal courts to put them in the penitentiary." *Lenske v. United States*, 383 F.2d 20 (9th Cir. 1967).

and Jewish educators from the area around Kovno, Lithuania. Jack was born in 1898, while Jean was born in London in 1899 where her father, Cantor Abraham Rosenbloom, served a congregation there on the family's way to America.

Close friends throughout their childhood, when Jean's parents moved to New York City so Abraham could accept a new cantorial assignment, she stayed in Minneapolis with Jack's family. Living quarters were tight, and Jean became the fifth person in the children's bedroom, where they all shared two beds. As my grandfather put it, propinquity took over, and the two teenagers, aged 17 and 16, became secret lovers. My grandmother ended up pregnant with my mother, and Jack and Jean went over the border into Wisconsin where the marriage laws were more lenient, and were secretly married by a justice of the peace.

My grandparents went back to their respective families not long after the marriage, and gradually grew apart. My grandmother was soon out of the house and singing in jazz clubs in New Orleans and Chicago, and my mother was raised by her two sets of grandparents, shuffled back and forth on the train between Minneapolis and New Orleans, Cantor Rosenbloom's next posting, during her childhood and adolescence.

My grandfather's parents were Meyer David ("M. D.") Mirviss and his wife Masha, and it was their children and grandchildren who were the extended family I knew best in my childhood. They fled Lithuania as a young couple in 1907 with Jack and his sister Rose to escape the same persecution of Jews that had driven my father's family out of Russia and Ukraine some years earlier. Their last four children were born in Minneapolis.

In Minneapolis M. D. worked as a peddler, selling a variety of goods door to door from a donkey cart. His best efforts, however, other than his family, were directed toward the Minneapolis Jewish community. He served first as the temporary rabbi at the Adath Jeshurun Synagogue, and then as its beloved *shamos* (sexton) and assistant rabbi for the next forty-eight years, filling in at every job from rabbi to janitor if necessary to cover vacancies, until his death in 1955.

In addition to M. D.'s religious duties he was a founder, organizer, or director of every significant Jewish organization in Minneapolis at the time, working tirelessly on humanitarian causes for the benefit of his community. I was too young to be aware of the specifics, but it was clear even to me that the extent of his efforts did not go unacknowledged. Committed Zionists at a time when that meant support for the new State of Israel, which had just been approved by the United Nations as a homeland for the Jewish people after the extermination of six million Jews by the Nazis in World War II, they were honored in 1949 by their appreciative congregation with a five-week trip to Israel. The next year, the Meyer D. and Masha Mirviss Chapel was dedicated at the second Adath Jeshurun Synagogue, walking distance from their small house. When I later read that in 1945 they had been feted at a reception in their honor on the occasion of their 50th wedding anniversary, I was not surprised by the news account that "[m]ore than 1,000 people attended the party...to greet the most beloved couple in the Northwest."[3]

Following in his father's footsteps, my grandfather Jack became a Jewish educator, the director of major Jewish community centers in Milwaukee and Minneapolis, and lastly, the Hillel director at Ohio University. He retired to Israel in his sixties, returning to the States to visit family in his seventies and eighties, often stopping off in Vermont to help us put our garden to bed. He lived to be 103, outdoing his mother Masha, who "only" lived to 101.

My parents met at the University of Minnesota and married shortly after my mother's graduation in 1937. After she became a wife and mother she worked on and off as family finances required, and in the family

---

[3] Etta Fay Orkin, *125 Years of Adath Jeshurun Congregation*, (IGI Publishing, 2009), 46.

tradition was a very active volunteer in the community. She co-founded and served as the general chairwoman of the free Rheumatic Fever Diagnostic Clinic, and served on the boards of Jewish Family Service, the Jewish Community Center, and Planned Parenthood of St. Paul. Over time she worked as a caseworker at St. Paul Family Service, the Ramsey County Welfare Board, and within the Minneapolis public school system. As a youngster I was very aware of these involvements and of the respect she garnered in the community.

My mother died in 1969 when I was just 23, and it took me a long while to realize the full extent of my loss. I came to regret terribly that I never had a chance to know her as an adult and to ask her all the questions I had about her childhood and upbringing, but she nonetheless taught me important lessons about the things that matter in life.

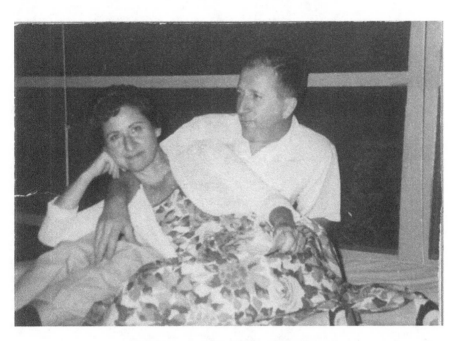

My parents, as I like to remember them.

Heading off for my first day of kindergarten at Horace Mann School, with brother Peter.

Chapter Three

Politics Gets Personal

The 1950s

My first political act was spinning a homemade wheel of fortune at a fundraising carnival for Henry A. Wallace held at our home in St. Paul in 1948. That year, when I was three, Wallace was a candidate for president of the United States on the Progressive Party ticket. A former secretary of agriculture, secretary of commerce, and vice president under Franklin D. Roosevelt, Wallace ran on a platform of reviving the New Deal, addressing segregation and discrimination, and ending the cold war with the Soviet Union.

The Midwest at the time was an important part of the country politically. These were the days of the great Midwestern populists—Wallace from Iowa and Robert "Bob" LaFollette from Wisconsin—and of the great postwar liberals, most notably Hubert Humphrey from Minnesota. My parents were supporting Wallace in 1948 and had agreed to host the fundraiser for him in our unfinished basement.

My father loved to tinker and had made a wheel of fortune for the carnival at his workbench downstairs. He wasn't an experienced woodworker, and it was pretty rough, but he knew how it needed to operate and it performed well. He coated the face of the wheel with glue, then sprinkled silver glitter all over it, and I thought it was one of the most wonderful things I'd ever seen. My job was to spin the wheel each time my father collected a ticket.

My brother found more interesting the set of four large caricatures of Harry Truman, Thomas Dewey, Harold Stassen, and Joseph Ball, which had been drawn on particle board by Minneapolis artist/activist Syd Fossum for a dart game concession. Peter struggled to understand why people were throwing darts at these men, but later in life as a political science major he figured it out, and the caricatures have hung in his study ever since.

The people who came and milled around in our basement that night were largely familiar to me. They were the same people my parents socialized with and who allowed me to toddle around them at my parents' cocktail parties, feeding me herring in tomato sauce on Ritz crackers and the first piece of pizza I ever ate, before sending me back up the hall to bed. They were people my parents had met and become active with at the University of Minnesota in the late 1930s when the state's left-leaning Farmer Labor Party (FLP) was dominant.

By 1944, however, the FLP had collapsed and its followers had mostly joined the Roosevelt-oriented Minnesota Democratic Party to form the Democratic Farmer Labor party, or "DFL" as it is still known today, electing Hubert Humphrey mayor of Minneapolis and launching his political career.

Those who couldn't stomach the merger or the way it had been achieved—which included my parents and their friends—became Progressive Party people and remained so until around 1950, when the party ceased to be an influential force. They then gravitated back to the DFL and made it one of the most progressive state Democratic organizations in the country. In addition to Humphrey, over the years the DFL contributed to the national scene such political personalities as Orville Freeman, Gene McCarthy, Walter (Fritz) Mondale, Don and Arvonne Fraser, and Paul Wellstone, and continues to do so today.

*   *   *

One of my favorite spots in our house as a toddler was the long built-in window seat in our living room, made of beautifully shellacked hardwood topped by a quilted brown pad with thin, shiny gold threads running through the fabric. Below the window seat ran a shelf that was endlessly entertaining, consisting of cupboards enclosed by little doors or left open as bookshelves.

Before I could read, most of the books on the shelves did not interest me. There were three exceptions: the many volumes of the red *World Book Encyclopedia*, with all its many pictures; the unabridged *Merriam Webster Dictionary*, remarkable for its extreme size and weight; and the two volumes of *The Letters of Lincoln Steffens,* the first matching books I'd ever seen other than the encyclopedia, and which I could tell were in a different class. I had no idea who Lincoln Steffens was, or what it was he had to say, but the embossed gold "I" and "II" on badly faded covers intrigued me. I wouldn't meet up with Steffens again until my college days when I studied U.S. intellectual history; when I learned he was a famous progressive muckraking journalist I understood why his *Letters* had been in our house.

The section of the shelf that had little doors on it housed a big box full of loose photographs, along with three black photo albums with covers trimmed in gold. Mostly the albums held pictures from my parents' two trips to Mexico, first on their honeymoon and again a few years later with close friends.

There was absolutely nothing in these pictures that I recognized or could relate to; yet they were obviously very important, having been carefully put away in the fancy albums. The houses were plain and cold looking, and clearly made of something different from ours; the people all had brown skin and dressed as if it were very hot; even the ground, the trees, and the shrubbery looked different, with hardly any grass. It all looked very barren and scorched.

The only things in my world that these photographs seemed to resemble were some larger pictures hanging on the walls of our home. Two of these were matching drawings of a very serious boy and girl, both with brown skin and big brown eyes staring out very somberly, I thought, from the wall in my parents' bedroom.

Three others were a set of small prints, also of brown-skinned people, but these people were crazily intertwined with each other in tree branches in one picture, gathering wheat together in another, and sleeping curled up with their children in the third.

Finally, a large print occupied the place of honor over the fireplace in our living room: a brown-skinned woman adjusting a huge basket of crops tied on the back of a brown-skinned man who was on his hands and knees. It was hard to tell if he was meant to crawl away with his burden or actually stand up with it on his back, but from the look of things both seemed almost impossible.

The large print, I later came to learn, was *El Cargador de Flores,* or *The Flower Carrier*, Diego Rivera's symbolic portrayal of the struggle of the working class, which he painted in 1935. The trio of smaller prints, also by Rivera, were from a larger fresco and included *La Noche de los Pobres*, or *Night of the Poor*. All of the prints had been brought back from Mexico by my parents, and somehow, even as a very small child, they came to symbolize in my mind the things my family cared about, though I couldn't have articulated what those were until I was much older. I eventually inherited the large print, which has hung everywhere I've lived.

*   *   *

In 1950, when I was in kindergarten at Horace Mann School, most elementary school children in neighborhood public schools like ours came home for lunch, because their stay-at-home mothers were there to feed them. One day after lunch I followed my brother back to school for the afternoon session before my mother realized I was gone. My teacher angrily turned me over to the principal, who scolded me as she drove me home, then lectured my mother in front of me for allowing me to do such a thing.

My mother, after apologizing for the inconvenience, defended me and lectured the principal right back for making me feel bad for wanting to go to school. She would defend my escapades and champion my causes throughout my childhood, repeatedly modeling important lessons about standing up to authority.

I completed kindergarten at Horace Mann but did not continue there. It was 1951 and U.S. Senator Joseph McCarthy was leading the charge against real and imagined Communists whom he was certain were infiltrating every aspect of American life, determined to destroy the country. The so-called "Red Scare" hysteria caught up with a woman who lived down the street from us, and she rose up at a PTA meeting one night to denounce my parents as Communists. This they were not, though they were still members of the Progressive Party, which was widely believed to include Communists.

This being the era of guilt by association, that was all our neighbors needed to hear. My parents felt the situation at Horace Mann had become untenable, and fearing reprisals or discriminatory treatment toward me and my brother, removed us from the St. Paul public school system, never to return.

Years later, when I was being victimized by anti-Semites for my civic and political leadership in Lincoln City, Oregon, our friend Laura Carper urged us to leave the community and find a more hospitable place to live. I argued vehemently that leaving meant giving in, letting the bigots win, and that such behavior would only encourage them. She had a different way of looking at it. "Stay long enough to win this battle if you must," she said, "but then get out. The children need to learn that they don't have to put up with that crap."

Apparently my parents had been of Laura's same opinion when they decided to remove us from Horace Mann, and I'm glad they were. I'm convinced that their decision to enroll us at the University of Minnesota's laboratory schools did no less than change the course of my life.

Once they decided to remove us from Horace Mann my parents had limited choices. This was long before parents had the option of charter schools, magnet schools, or transferring their children to another neighborhood school. There were other private schools in St. Paul that in theory our parents could have chosen, but most were affiliated with the Catholic church, or catered to a wealthier, more privileged, and largely Protestant population. Wealthy and privileged—as that word was used at the time to mean rich, white, and Protestant—were not words that would have been used to describe our family.

Our parents had several close friends who taught or were on staff at the U, and whose children attended the university's lab schools; that, I'm sure, had a major part in their decision to send us there. It was a definite choice but not without drawbacks. There was tuition to pay, and parents had to ferry their children all over the Twin Cities if they were going to maintain class friendships, at least until we were old enough to drive.

I started at UES in the first grade; my brother was in fourth. At UES there was one class at each grade level, consisting of twenty-five students. Many were the children of professors who taught at the U; the rest of us were a hodgepodge of "others" from all over the Twin Cities, whose parents, for one reason or another, thought it a good place for us.

PTA meetings at UES must have been refreshing for my parents. Instead of the red-baiting neighbors at Horace Mann, the parents of many of my new classmates were political and cultural leaders from around the Twin Cities.[4] They were DFLers all, and many were personal friends of Hubert Humphrey.

Our parents explained that we were now going to a "public-private" school. Try as we might, neither Peter nor I ever figured out what a "public-private" school was, but whenever one of our neighborhood friends asked us what kind of a school we went to that required our taking an orange school bus from the corner of Cretin and Scheffer, we'd say that anybody could go there, so it was public, but you had to pay, so it was private. They looked at us like we were nuts and the explanation never made much sense to us either.

Years later, when I was a parent myself, and our daughter Elizabeth was about to start school in Vermont, we were contacted by a small group of parents from our area who were starting a private school nearby, to see if we'd be interested in enrolling our kids. I'm embarrassed to say now that I gave the caller quite a self-righteous lecture over the phone about the importance of public education and our strong commitment to it. At the time I didn't give a thought to the fact that I hadn't had a public education myself, nor that Jim had spent his last two years of high school at The Newton School, a tiny private farm-based school in South Windham, Vermont. I was speaking from a political philosophy that hadn't yet been tested.

---

[4] My classmates' parents included Maurice Visscher, chair of the U's Department of Physiology, known for its liberal and humanistic faculty; Robert and Maeve Beck, he a professor of the History and Philosophy of Education and she an authority on Virginia Woolf; Dick and Roz Kleeman, he a reporter and later editor of the *Minneapolis Tribune* and she a staffer for Hubert Humphrey, who herself had been instrumental in the founding of the DFL; Don and Meg Torbert, he a professor of Art History, she an artist and curator at the Walker Art Center; Herman Ramras from the U's German Department; Frank Whiting, director of theatre at the U; and Fran and Art Naftalin, she who would preside over the Minneapolis Library Board for many years and he then on Humphrey's staff, and later the mayor of Minneapolis from 1961-1969.

But by third grade Elizabeth had become a school dropout, often feigning illness and refusing to go to school. After repeated teacher conferences failed to improve things, we reluctantly enrolled her at Riverside, the school our friends had started. In just a single year there her academic life was saved by Riverside's small classes, mixed age groups, experiential learning philosophy, and creative, caring teachers.

She went back to public school when we moved to Oregon the following year, then finished eighth grade at the St Johnsbury Middle School when we returned to Vermont in the fall of 1993, doing very well at both places and entering high school as a confident and successful student.

Our son Daniel had a different problem. He had a very retentive mind and excelled in the classroom without hardly trying. As early as first grade he was particularly interested in geography. We were not surprised when he tested as talented and gifted at his elementary school in Oregon. But he was a shy boy, and firmly refused the special summer programs that were suggested, where he'd have to engage with children and adults he didn't know.

When we returned to St. Johnsbury from Oregon, Daniel was about to begin fourth grade, and I inquired what might be available at the St. Johnsbury School to challenge him and explore his interests. When the principal's reluctant but truthful answer was essentially "nothing," we enrolled *him* at Riverside, where, as a fourth grader, he had a grand time indulging his interest in geography, and came in third in the Vermont State Geography Bee competing against seventh and eighth graders.

Daniel loved and excelled at Riverside through 8th grade, when he followed Elizabeth into St. Johnsbury Academy, itself a private school to which the Town of St. Johnsbury pays tuition for its high school students.

Having reluctantly sent one and then the other of my own children to a private elementary school with great feelings of guilt at having abandoned the public school system, I suspect that my parents, in telling us we were going to a "public-private" school, were probably expressing some of that same guilt, needing to justify their decision to themselves.

I don't pretend to know the answer to this conundrum. There are many students in the public school system who, because of their unique needs or the poor quality of their local school, need and deserve a better education than they are getting, but lack the school funding, personal funding, or effective parental advocacy, to make it happen. There is no getting around the fact that my children were privileged in this regard, as were my brother and I. Yes, we needed scholarship help to send our children to Riverside, and it's quite likely the same was true of my parents when they sent us to the university schools, but in both cases we were able to make it happen.

I have never doubted that all parents, whatever their own educational background or station in life, want the best education they can get for their children, but so many are unable to obtain it, and the rest of us, collectively, have failed to take responsibility for making sure that every child's education helps them develop their full potential.

*   *   *

I took the orange school bus to UES and then U-High for twelve years. I was bused fifteen miles each way, the equivalent in time to two class periods. It certainly didn't do me any harm, if you don't count freezing your toes waiting for a bus to appear during a Minnesota winter.

In my later years, if for some reason I had to stay late at school for a club meeting or event, I had to take the city bus home. At that time of day nearly all of the passengers were private or parochial high school students. In the space of one mile as we approached my own neighborhood, the uniformed girls from the Summit School, Our Lady of Peace, and Derham Hall got on at a series of stops, together with the boys from St. Thomas

Academy, the College of St. Thomas, and Cretin, all very serious in their military garb, plus the boys from St. Paul Academy in their preppy jackets and ties. Unlike the camaraderie we enjoyed on our orange UES/U-High bus, practically every minute of these trips was intimidating.

I never really thought through my childhood bus-riding experiences until I was an adult, but it always felt like I lived in a somewhat awkward neighborhood. St. Paul at the time had the highest proportion of Catholics of any city in the country except Boston. As a child growing up in Highland Park I was surrounded by Catholics, but knew very few.

As a younger child the only place I really came into contact with Catholics was at the Meeks' skating rink up the block. The Meeks family had six children, and owned an undeveloped lot on our block next to their house. Every winter Mr. Meeks—with the help of an older child or two—flooded the empty lot and allowed anyone to skate there if the Meeks boys weren't practicing hockey.

The other noticeable group in our neighborhood were the other Jews, who also seemed to be a significant bloc, particularly after the woods were cleared and the Temple of Aaron built. Like the Catholics they also seemed to stick together and busy their children with after-school faith-based activities and youth groups.

The Protestants were definitely in the minority. As a child I had no idea who they were, where they went to school, or what they did that was different, until as a budding teenager my mother sent me to take an errant piece of mail to 560 Mt. Curve Boulevard, accidentally delivered to us at 650. There I met Sara Murphy, who became one of my closest friends through high school and into college, and who introduced me to the families of other Protestant friends of hers, who seemed very similar to our own.

Twenty years later I read an article in the *New York Times* about the fire-bombing of a Planned Parenthood clinic just six blocks from the house I grew up in. Abortion services were being performed there along with other family planning services, and the facility had been under steady attack since it had been in the planning stages. It was the only time I've ever read about my neighborhood in the national media, and there were no surprises.

*　　　　　*　　　　　*

In 1952, everyone in my family favored Adlai Stevenson for president and was very excited about his candidacy. Everyone, that is, but me. I was a staunch supporter of Dwight D. Eisenhower for reasons I don't recall, except that I thought he was a nice grandfatherly looking man. About to turn seven, I surely wasn't conducting any deeper political analysis, and in retrospect I can't imagine any other reason. My brother, then ten, gave me a hard time about it, but my parents wisely let me find my own way.

My fall garb at that age rarely changed from sneakers, blue jeans, and a child-sized warm-up jacket, shiny maroon with gold sleeves and trim and brass snaps up the front—the U of M colors. That fall I plastered the front of my jacket with Eisenhower buttons in all sizes, including a four-inch-diameter beauty with a picture of a benevolently smiling Ike on it.

One Saturday I went downtown with my family wearing the jacket, and after doing other errands, my father, brother, and I presented ourselves at Stevenson headquarters to pick up my mother, where she was doing campaign work. My arrival caused a sensation and my mother took a serious ribbing, but never then, nor at any other time I can remember, was I ever pressured to think a certain way just because my parents did. Both parents served as examples in many ways and in many areas, but my choices were always my own.

*　　　　　*　　　　　*

My elementary school years were full ones in traditional and nontraditional ways. On Saturday mornings I took classes at the YWCA: one was a combination of ballet, tap dance, and gymnastics; the other was dramatics.

Ballet and tap didn't really interest me, but I loved gymnastics, which surprised no one, as I was very athletic and deeply involved in many sports. In first and second grade I played football at recess—the only girl who did—and the boys allowed it, because though small I was very fast. I often and proudly wore my shoulder pads on the school bus on those crisp fall football mornings. This continued until my brother broke his leg playing football in fifth grade, and my parents made me stop, which seemed a very misplaced reaction.

I was also very good at baseball, and insisted on trying out for Little League when I was old enough. My father supported me in this and took me to the tryouts, but this was the mid-1950s and he probably knew all along that they wouldn't let me try out, let alone join a team.

While I am happy that Title IX has given girls and young women today the sports opportunities denied me, I have to confess that I harbor to this day some sadness that it came too late for me. Athletics was an area where I excelled as a child. I think I might have made a serious mark, but the opportunities just weren't there.

Dramatics was another story. Whenever the U of M's theatre program needed children to play roles in a university production, UES was the first place they looked. A classmate's father was director of the U's Theatre Department, and I'm sure that didn't hurt our chances, along with the fact that we were conveniently nearby right on campus for late-afternoon rehearsals.

The entire school routinely attended en masse all of the productions of the Young People's University Theatre twice a year. It was thrilling to sit in the Scott Hall auditorium, surrounded by young people from other Twin

City schools, listening with rapt attention as Kenneth Graham and his puppet Skippy talked to us about what a theatre was, how you were supposed to act when you were in one, and what that day's play was about.

As I attended the Scott Hall performances, I longed to be an active part of them. My chance came in fifth grade, when I was cast as the youngest child in the U's operatic production of Benjamin Britten's "The Little Chimney Sweep," aka "Let's Make an Opera." Joanne Jonson, a graduate student in theatre was our director, and every moment was a thrill, from the auditions to the two-hour rehearsals, to the shows themselves, including one out of town in St. Cloud. This was my debut on a major stage, and the first of a lifetime of presentations and performances.

A related opportunity came, beginning in fourth grade, with the introduction of a foreign language to our studies. UES offered French, Spanish, and German instruction in rotation, and that year German was taught; I unquestioningly studied the German language for the next eleven years. I apparently attained an early proficiency, for while I was still in grade school I was invited to be part of a radio show, *Gesundheit!* written by Lotte Seidler, which was broadcast live from KUOM, the U of M's radio station. Combined with my theatre work I have no doubt that this added to my sense of myself as a person who could be expected to perform well in public.

There are many other things I remember fondly about UES that undoubtedly contributed to my later political activism. One I hadn't thought much about until I went back for a reunion was the library. Throughout my UES days I spent many happy free periods sitting on the library floor reading through the collection, my favorites being a series of biographies of famous Americans such as Abraham Lincoln, Booker T. Washington, George Washington Carver, and Jane Addams. I loved to read, and it was there that I first learned how very ordinary people who felt strongly about something could actually do something about it when they grew up. The seed was planted.

*   *   *

My summers were spent at summer camp, first at day camp and then, starting when I was six, at overnight camp every summer for six years straight. In retrospect, my camp experiences seem to have had three purposes: to occupy me in the summer, to provide some respite for my parents, and to bolster my Jewish identity and education without the family having to join a temple or synagogue or otherwise take part in organized religious activities, which my parents didn't believe in.

My grandfather Jack and his second wife, Lillian, had fulfilled a longtime dream of theirs by purchasing an estate on Kabol Lake in northern Wisconsin in 1951. They turned it into Camp Gan Eden, a small Jewish summer camp for girls. Even though I was only six the year it opened, my parents had no qualms about sending me there to spend the entire summer as a camper, and I spent three happy summers there and three more summers at Jewish camps elsewhere after that. I loved overnight camp and developed a Jewish identity at the same time.

It seems a little odd that my parents would want to have immersed me so much in Jewish culture and observances since we paid little attention to either at home, but in retrospect I think they may simply have been preparing me for my future as a Jew in a Gentile world, with my own children to raise, educate, and guide through whatever they might encounter because they were Jews. After all, while I was being raised as a secular Jew, I was also born in the immediate aftermath of the Holocaust, where such distinctions as "observant" vs "secular" were of no relevance to the fate a Jew would suffer. And, as I would be reminded over and over again throughout my life, anti-Semitism remains alive and well everywhere.

Raising my own children with a Jewish identity was harder for me than it was for my parents. For one thing, ours is a mixed marriage, and with most of my family on the other side of the country, I've never had anyone on hand to help me recreate the family-centered holiday celebrations of my childhood. Thankfully, Jim went peaceably along with every scheme I came up with to instill in the kids a sense of their Jewishness and some knowledge of what that meant. They attended a combined Sunday school/Hebrew school once a week for a year or so, as I had done. When we had the time and money to travel, we commonly used it to visit my relatives, often to join in an event with Jewish content, like a bar mitzvah or Passover seder. Elizabeth, chafing under the conservatism of St. Johnsbury Academy, chose to do a semester of her junior year at the Alexander Muss High School in Israel, where she was bat mitzvahed at the end of the program. That same year, when Daniel was thirteen, he and I travelled to Israel where he prepared for and celebrated his bar mitzvah at Kibbutz Urim under his great-grandfather's supervision. So, although we lived a fairly isolated existence in northern Vermont, both children understood from an early age that they were part of a much larger family, and that my half of that family was Jewish.

But most of their elementary school years the kids were the only Jews in their classrooms, or nearly the only ones, which led well-intentioned teachers to invite me in to talk to the class about Chanukah, and do a little show-and-tell with *menorahs* and *dreidls*. This is always a fraught undertaking for Jewish parents, and many of us who do it do so with misgivings, knowing that at best it is likely to embarrass our children and label them as "different" in their classmates' eyes, just when they are longing to fit in.

Still, I don't think I ever declined such an invitation because ignorance about the Jewish religion and Jews was so rampant in our community—to the point where I sometimes felt I might scream if I heard Chanukah referred to as "the Jewish Christmas" one more time, or heard a Chanukah song sung at what was billed as the elementary school's "Christmas Concert."

I spoke up about these things repeatedly to teachers, principals, superintendents, and town officials, because I have always felt very strongly that in addition to the poor ethics of it, the Constitution guarantees to my children, and everyone else's children, a right to feel, when they attend their public school and participate in its events, that the school belongs to them as much as it belongs to anyone.

Similarly, I, and anyone else who does not celebrate Christian holidays, ought to be able to enter their town office and do business with town officials in December without having to feel that the town is not quite as much there for them as it is for others, as evidenced by the Christmas decorations allowed to grace the walls of many town offices each year.

Unfortunately, most of my conversations with school and town administrators over the years have elicited apologies, but no changes in behavior. But I did have one success, and it still makes me smile when I drive past the St. Johnsbury Town School in December, and see that the light bulbs in the all-glass entryway have been changed out *not* in favor of the red and green bulbs that replaced them the first year the new school opened, but with light bulbs of many different colors that make every child who goes to school there feel like it's a festive month for them.

I have come to the conclusion that most people simply can't walk in someone else's shoes. If they tried, they would quickly realize their own privilege as a member of the majority. Until you *are* a minority person that's being treated differently, whether it be treatment based on race, religion, disability, gender, or sexual orientation, and whether it be intentional or malicious or not, you simply cannot understand how the

36

sometimes very subtle things that bring great pleasure and joy to the majority convey to a minority person that they do not belong.

With Peter, 1961

Chapter Four

Developing Context

1957-1963

I started at University High School—U-High—in the fall of 1957. The class I was to be a part of for the next six years was different from my UES class, yet the same. Our numbers expanded from twenty-five to seventy-five and the demographics changed some, but the essence of the experience was very similar. While about a third of the class now came from the largely blue-collar neighborhood of St. Anthony in northeast Minneapolis, which lacked a high school of its own, there was also a new influx of students from Prospect Park, the small, tightly-knit residential area just east of the U of M campus, where many professors and their families lived.

The children of the academics continued to dominate the school culture, as they had at UES. The St. Anthony kids at least had each other. We "others" were still a very geographically scattered group, fitting in where and how we could, depending on our individual abilities and interests. As a result, I developed an ability to make do without a ready-made clique of my own, and I think because of that, have never since had a close group of friends with whom I am in regular contact, nor the sense of permanent belonging it provides.

Fortunately, the school as a whole did foster the feeling of being part of a strong, cohesive community. There were a few things that seventh and eighth graders didn't participate in or had their own parallel activity for, but for the most part we were a single, small student body of students in grades 7-12, sharing the same hallways and classrooms, sitting together in assemblies, and cheering for the same teams. We were encouraged to get to know each other, and seniors were matched as "big brothers" or "big sisters" with seventh graders, giving each of us our own special connection with the older students. A fair number of academic classes also mixed students from different grade levels, so everyone could learn at their own pace.

The mixing of age and grade levels made it a particular advantage to have a brother three years older. I knew those of Peter's friends who visited our house, and in keeping with the school culture they were comfortable acknowledging me in the halls. This gave me a little boost in stature, at least in my own eyes. And it wasn't a phenomenon restricted to those of us with older siblings. For example, when the Soviet Union launched Sputnik on October 4, 1957—the first manmade object to orbit the earth—a senior five years ahead of me in school, who had apparently been observing my general level of activity, bestowed on me the nickname "Sputnik." It stuck with his group of friends, who enjoyed hailing me by that name when we crossed paths.

One of the events that brought all of the grades together, at least the female half of them—probably in answer to the annual athletic banquet, which at that time was all male—was the annual mother-daughter banquet, held in the University of Minnesota's Coffman Memorial Union ballroom on the far side of the campus from U-High. At the end of our seventh-grade year I was selected to speak at the banquet on behalf of my class. It felt like a very big deal. The room was very fancy, as befits the main ballroom of a major university, and the audience was 450 girls and their mothers, plus female faculty and administrators. It was the first time I sat at a head table and the first time I gave a speech.

Four years later, as a junior, I chaired the speakers' committee that handled arrangements for the banquet speakers, and introduced them. My brother was studying overseas then, and my mother wrote him, "Dinah introduced each speaker and did a very good job of it—with no preparation. She holds an audience's attention and says appropriate things. What can you do with this talent, we wondered, run for political office? Not such a sound basis for good government."

I didn't see this letter until many years later when my brother sent me a packet of letters he had received from our parents while in Germany. My mother's letters were full of surprises. It was clear that she had held a rather poor opinion of me at the time as a feckless, boy-crazy teenager, which certainly didn't fit my opinion of myself at that time and hurt me to discover. Even her assumption that I had not prepared for my role as speakers' committee chair but had simply done a good job off the cuff was far from what I felt to be the truth. I have always been an *over*-preparer, but apparently did not share those efforts with her.

My activities those first couple of years at U-High were focused on athletics, for which I now at least had an outlet in the Girls' Recreation Association, the swim team, and as a cheerleader for the 7th- and 8th-grade boys' teams. Even physical education classes were a significant opportunity, as being on the U of M campus gave us access to the university's pool and golf course, in addition to our very own gym across the street.

Student elections and mock elections that paralleled significant state and national elections were taken very seriously as learning experiences at our school, and were my introduction to the behind-the-scenes work involved in electoral politics. Mock election campaigns went on for a week or more and included speeches and debates, development of campaign materials, and election day rallies. Younger students were as involved in these activities as older students, and it was no wonder that our class in particular took to it from the start, as we had an unusually high number of politically well-placed parents.[5] As little as we knew about the real issues underlying political choices in our early U-high years, all we had to do was observe our parents and our friends' parents to know from a young age the importance politics was likely to play in our lives.

In 1956 Adlai Stevenson ran for president again. This time I was on the same side as the rest of my family and pretty much everyone else we knew. I couldn't fathom the possibility that he wouldn't win, but of course he didn't, losing to Dwight Eisenhower again. I was stunned. It was the first time I had cared—*really* cared—about an election, and I couldn't believe that the person I supported —the *right* person—hadn't won. How could that be? I would have the experience of being on the losing side many times over in the future, and as I got older I came to accept it even if I often still didn't understand it very well, but that first time was really rough.

I started ninth grade in the fall of 1959 and as the '60s began, with all the social, political, and cultural upheaval that the decade brought, and as my reach beyond my immediate family expanded, so too did my awareness and grasp of political events, and their importance in my life.

In October 1960, a politically active parent of one of my classmates had a brilliant idea: Why not invite the kids to come work at the state DFL's annual Bean Feed fundraiser at the Minneapolis Auditorium? Presidential candidate John F. Kennedy was to be the main speaker, and it was clear to our parents that many of us were already as politically interested as they

---

[5]Added to the already impressive list of politically active parents of my UES classmates when we got to U-High were Cy Barnum, professor of physiologic chemistry at the U, who was active in the Fair Play for Cuba Committee; John Williams, professor of physics at the U and an appointee to the U.S. Atomic Energy Commission; Orville Freeman, governor of Minnesota from 1955-1961, then U.S. secretary of agriculture under Presidents Kennedy and Johnson; Jane Freeman, a DFL organizer and political activist on many fronts; and Elliot Roosevelt, son of FDR. See also note 4.

were. We jumped at the chance, for Kennedy had ignited the imagination of a majority of the country by then, and its young people in particular; we were no exception. We did our assigned jobs and were rewarded with ringside seats on the floor for Kennedy's speech.

I have always found one of the few advantages of my size to be my ability to get through large crowds without incurring anyone's wrath. People seem to look at me and take pity, immediately knowing that I won't be able to see a thing unless they step aside and let me through. Somehow, once Kennedy finished speaking, I ended up on stage with a massive group of people congratulating him and shaking his hand. I was lucky enough to meet him and get his autograph on a folded-up piece of paper that someone took from their pocket and thrust at me at just the right moment. I donated it years later for a fundraising auction sponsored by my local Democratic committee, and have been sorry ever since, as many in that group found me too far to the left for their taste when I later ran for office, and gave me only lukewarm support when I needed much more to win.

My personal experience with electoral politics during my high school years was confined to running for the Student Senate each year, at which I was successful as a junior and senior, and working on other people's campaigns. Although I was active in many other extracurricular activities, I was never the one who made it to the very top of the things that were important to me. Yet I survived my failures with my ego intact by dipping into the well of resilience that was in my genes, and found other ways to feel good about myself.

I had been a "C" squad cheerleader in 8th grade and made the "B" squad as a junior, but didn't make the "A" squad as a senior and suffered from it none too silently. Nonetheless, I presided over the Girls' Recreation Association and helped it develop into a sought-after activity that was both healthy and fun.

My interest in dramatics also continued and I was inducted into Thespians as a senior in recognition of years of behind-the-scenes work; but I never appeared in a play at U-High. Undaunted, I took my interest to community theatre at Theatre St. Paul, where as a sophomore in high school I was cast in a production of *Snow White*.

I was a good writer and worked on the yearbook in addition to being class editor of our literary magazine my junior year, but failed to be named one of the editors of either publication as a senior, taking comfort in the fact that a long article I wrote my senior year explaining the ins and outs of U-High to the general public was accepted and published with a byline in the *St. Paul Pioneer Press*.

I got good grades in high school, but the year I graduated half the class had a B average or better, so although the school had to honor twice as many graduates as usual, that didn't include me. I don't remember being at all jealous of my classmates' academic honors; most of the rest of us were just proud of how unusually smart and interesting our class was, by almost any measure.

I am certain that my failure to reach the top when I wanted to and my resilience in the face of defeat were key features of the self I developed in these early years, a self that never gave up. That self was also gradually acquiring a set of skills and abilities that would stand me in good stead when I entered public life: comfort with radio and on stage, the ability to address large groups of people, and above all, organizational skills.

I was always in the middle of things, honing my organizational skills behind the scenes. These skills came to fruition when I chaired the two biggest assemblies held my senior year: the Senior Assembly, and the first ever (maybe only ever) Folksong Assembly, which I conceived and organized. Having an older brother had put me in touch early on with the developing music of the Sixties, and as a high school student I was increasingly drawn to the growing folk music movement, from the Kingston

Trio to Pete Seeger to Minnesotan Bob Dylan—then Bobby Zimmerman—who was playing at coffee houses around the U along with our schoolmate Dave Ray, who was teaming up with Tony Glover and "Spider" John Koerner to make interesting music of a sort I'd never heard before, called bluegrass.

My high school organizing sometimes had a decidedly real-world political thread. Taking advantage of the fact that we were in the midst of a college campus, I was a member of the U of M Student Peace Union by the time I was a senior, and a classmate and I attempted to organize a chapter at U-High. As a recruiting device we distributed flyers for an event being held at the U's Coffman Memorial Union, where the SPU was sponsoring a talk by a well-known communist, Gus Hall, on the growing civil rights and antiwar movements.

The response of the U-High administration to this was enlightening, if not enlightened. The principal refused to grant us a club charter, and the chair of the English Department took it upon himself to instigate a search of our lockers to see what other subversive materials we might be harboring. I'm sure to his disappointment there were none. We were simply already involved in adult politics. At the end of our senior year the student newspaper, the *Campus Breeze,* predicted the seniors' futures. My friend Marty was seen as destined to be arrested on a Freedom Walk, and I to get arrested picketing for her release.

North Carolina civil rights leader Quinton Baker introduces himself and "Project Understanding"

Courthouse where Griffin v Prince Edward County litigation began

Floyd McKissick of CORE explains school integration's likely timetable

Ku Klux Klan parade, Raleigh, North Carolina, April, 1965

Chapter Five

There's No One Way to Skin a Cat

1963-1967

I applied to two colleges, the University of Minnesota and the University of Wisconsin, and it was not until many years later that I began to wonder why that was so. My brother Peter, who had the same IQ and got the same grades in high school as I did, had also applied to and been accepted at two colleges, but the options for him were Stanford and Brown. He went off to Stanford in the fall of 1960 but didn't like it there, and after two years decided to finish his undergraduate work at the University of Minnesota.

Why my choices were so much more pedestrian I do not know. Perhaps it was sexism on the part of my guidance counselor, who may have felt that going to the best possible school I could get into was less important for me; or, perhaps the fact that Peter was not happy at Stanford suggested to my parents that farther away and more costly was not necessarily better. Most likely, the family finances at the time precluded a more expensive college education for me. In any case, I was anxious to go away from home after being on the U of M campus for twelve years, so I was happy with my acceptance at Wisconsin and the in-state tuition scholarship that came with it. Without giving it much more thought I arranged to live in a small, private dormitory on the shore of Lake Mendota called Lake Lawn Hall.

There were only about thirty of us living at Lake Lawn, which looked to be an old fraternity or sorority house that had seen better days. Most of the girls living there were from the East Coast. However, the roommate I was matched with was an observant Catholic from a small town in Indiana with whom I had nothing in common. She came from a family that was very conservative socially and politically. We got along fine, but that was the long and the short of it. When I got my ears pierced, she felt I had ruined my life and said so, bursting into tears at the sight of me when I got back to the dorm sporting gold studs. But she wasn't a mean person at all, and later felt badly about her outburst, apologizing and presenting me with a pair of earrings.

My two best friends my freshman year lived just down the hall from me—Jane Ehrlich, from Weston, Connecticut, and her roommate Carla Dalton, from Valley Stream, Long Island. I visited both at their homes during my college years, and became friendly with their families. They were well suited to each other, both being bright, hip, and politically radical, not to mention secular Jews like me.

I was immediately drawn to them. They had a level of East Coast sophistication that was entirely new to me in people my age, and which was very exciting. Had they not been required to live on campus their freshman year I'm sure they would have been happier elsewhere, so I considered the policy to be my very good luck. Jane would move to northern Vermont with her husband Carl a few years after we graduated, and remain a close friend.

I was at UW-Madison from the fall of 1963 to the winter of 1966. There couldn't have been a better time or place for me to have landed as a college freshman ready to cut her teeth as a political activist. Civil rights activism by college students had reached its peak in the early '60s when I was still in high school, but many UW students were still active in the difficult and dangerous ongoing voter registration drives being conducted in the

South, and shared a growing impatience with racial discrimination in the North.

Carl, a year ahead of us in school, had already been to the South when Jane met him as a freshman. His cousin was the head of UW Friends of SNCC, the Student Non-Violent Coordinating Committee, so we were quickly connected to what was happening in the activist community. I volunteered at a Freedom School in Milwaukee during the 1964-65 school boycotts there, teaching academic subjects, co-leading discussions about the meaning of freedom, and leading songs. I also worked on a drive for emergency medical supplies to support SNCC's participation in the Selma-to-Montgomery march on Bloody Sunday, and repeatedly attended demonstrations anywhere within my reach, including the August 1965 Assembly of Unrepresented People in Washington, D.C., my first national protest. I felt I was involved in critically important work for the first time, and it gave real-life meaning to my otherwise somewhat unreal existence as a college student.

In the fall of my sophomore year, I decided to look for a part-time job in order to cover that part of my tuition that wasn't paid by my scholarship, and ended up in a secretarial job with the Campus YWCA. I was familiar with the Y from my childhood classes, but at the time knew nothing about the breadth or depth of its social justice mission. I quickly learned that the Madison Y—like many other campus branches of the YW and YM national organizations—was deeply involved in social justice and anti-poverty work as a sponsor of programs and work/study opportunities for college students, and as a meeting place for activist student groups.

But my association with the Y almost didn't happen. In the course of being hired I was given a packet of information that made it clear that the YWCA was very much a Christian organization, something rather obvious from its full name but not from its acronym, which I'd never given much thought to. If I accepted the job, I would have to sign a form pledging my commitment to the organization's Christian mission.

I was seized with uncertainty about whether I could take the job with this condition, and called my mother to talk it out with her on the phone. She had no objection to my working at the Y, and felt that if I didn't either, that was all there was to it. As for the document I had to sign, she suggested I discuss it with my supervisor and see what she suggested. In the end I signed the document, being quite comfortable that the mission it spelled out—except for the Christian reference—was something I wholeheartedly believed in.

I quickly became a member of the Y's advisory board as well as an employee, and in April 1965 was asked to represent the organization on a University-sponsored trip to the South over spring vacation involving forty student leaders of campus organizations. Our mission was to see how school integration was faring in the South. In order to go I had to give up a previously planned trip to an antiwar demonstration in Washington, but I'd never been to the South and felt I needed this experience in order to speak about civil rights from a place of at least some personal knowledge.

We traveled by bus first to Prince Edward County, Virginia, then to Durham and Raleigh, North Carolina, on a fact-finding mission organized by UW student and Chapel Hill, North Carolina civil rights leader, Quinton Baker. Shortly after the bus left Madison, Baker introduced himself to us: A native of Greenville, North Carolina, a tobacco town, he grew up resentful of the limitations imposed on him by his race and became active in the civil rights movement during his first year at North Carolina College after he was refused permission to attend a Fred Waring concert. He saw the civil rights movement as a way to change how he could interact with the world, and was soon head of the student NAACP chapter, leading demonstrations and sit-ins in Durham and Chapel Hill. He had been recently paroled after serving time in prison for his role in a Chapel Hill protest that turned violent, and was able to take our group to North Carolina only by special permission from the governor.

In our time on the road with Baker, we learned as much about the state of school integration in the South as we'd have learned in a semester of academic study, and learned it in a way that has been impossible to forget.

With its ruling in *Brown v. Board of Education of Topeka*,[6] the U.S. Supreme Court had, in 1954, overturned the doctrine of "separate but equal" education for black and white children, which had been the law since 1896. This led to various efforts on the part of the Southern states to avoid the intent of the ruling: school integration. Virginia's response was to shutter all of its schools and make school attendance voluntary, thus avoiding the need to spend any money bringing schools serving black children up to existing standards for white students. The white population then developed a system of private school education to serve their children, leaving black children without any formal education at all.

Finally, in 1963, the Supreme Court in *Griffin v. Prince Edward County Board of Education* put a stop to Virginia's systematic evasion of *Brown*.[7] *Griffin* held that when the express purpose of closing schools was to deny education to a group of children based on race, it violated the Fourteenth Amendment's guarantee of equal protection; the defendant board of education was ordered to open the county's schools to all children.

Although the *Griffin* ruling seems like ancient history now, it had been handed down less than two years before our fact-finding trip south. Early in our trip we visited the courtroom where *Griffin* began. We then went on to see for ourselves what the effect of the Supreme Court decision had so far been.

---

[6] 347 US 483 (1954)
[7] 377 US 218 (1964)

We visited six historically black colleges and some elementary schools for black children still located in churches, and poorly equiped. We were headquartered at Shaw University, an all-black college in Raleigh founded in 1865, where I was horrified to see what our hosts had to put up with in order to get a college education: dilapidated dormitories with uncomfortable iron beds and rusty, inadequate plumbing; labs with next to no scientific equipment; outdated textbooks that had to be left in the classroom at the end of each class so they could be used by the next class coming in, if indeed there were any textbooks at all. It wasn't surprising to learn that Shaw had been the incubator where SNCC got its start. What *was* surprising was how clueless I had been about what college life was like for people my age but with a different skin color, just trying to get the same education I had.

We met extensively with civil rights and political leaders, including Floyd McKissick, the first African American student at the University of North Carolina School of Law at Chapel Hill, who was in line to become the next leader of CORE, the Congress of Racial Equality; and Governor Terry Sanford, who had just left office earlier that year. We quizzed them about what the future would hold for black students in the South, and when real change might occur.

On a break one day I walked downtown with my host from Shaw, a young black male student about my age. We were walking along on the sidewalk, lost in conversation, when a shot rang out and a bullet grazed the building right next to us. It took me a second to comprehend what had just happened, but my more experienced host yelled "run" and pushed me hard in the direction away from him, and I ran as fast as I could; he ran the other way even faster, and eventually we met back at the school. "Just trying to scare us," was the explanation. Well, they succeeded.

Another day we watched the Ku Klux Klan parade through downtown Raleigh, crowds lining the street on both sides cheering on the

Klan members parading in brightly colored satin regalia, accompanied by their security detail in military-style garb. Somehow it was even arranged for those of us who were white to attend an outdoor rally of the Klan that night, which required that we be dropped off a considerable distance away so that the cars we had come in wouldn't be identified. Vehicles of all sorts lined the rural road to the field where people of all ages had congregated. Klan members dressed in their white hooded cloaks cheered on one racist speaker after another.

I had of course heard about the Klan and its activities, but seeing it in action was another thing altogether. Part of me hoped I was on a movie set; it was terribly confusing that I was present at this hate-filled spectacle that was unfolding before my eyes—it made me feel physically ill and I wanted it not to be real. I was particularly struck by the young children wearing what seemed to be white pillowcases, who could not have understood much of what was happening other than the simple message they were being given that Negroes were bad people and they should hate them. The trip was a learning experience, that's for sure.

At this time the movement opposing the war in Vietnam was nascent, but growing rapidly, and the University of Wisconsin was a hotbed of anti-war activity. During my two and a half years at UW the movement to end the war in Vietnam was my main political involvement. In April 1965 I wrote a friend, "I don't feel as if I've been going to school at all this year, just sort of taking tests now and then, socializing a lot, and participating in political activities….Vietnam is almost all that's discussed here...at a teach-in we held last Thursday night an estimated 2000 people showed up! Fantastic."[8]

The anti-war activities I was involved in included teach-ins to educate the campus community as well as the greater community of Madison about the history of Vietnam and U.S. involvement there; citywide

---

[8] Letter from the author to Nancy Kleeman, April 3, 1965.

petition drives calling on Wisconsin's congressional delegation, as well as President Lyndon Johnson, to get the U.S. out of Vietnam; frequent local demonstrations at one strategic location or another; and of course weekend trips with busloads of other students and faculty heading for larger protests in Washington, D.C. demanding an end to the war.

Peter came to Madison in the fall of my sophomore year, having graduated from the University of Minnesota in May and decided to enroll at UW to work on a master's degree in political science. Both of us were involved with the UW Committee to End the War in Vietnam—Peter writing articles and giving speeches, me marching, attending rallies, and going door to door through Madison with educational literature and petitions. This was not all fun and games. In addition to the seriousness of the work itself, the UW campus and downtown Madison where the capitol is located lie between two lakes, Monona and Mendota. And while September and October are beautiful and April and May quite lovely, being outside during the months in between can be pretty raw. I remember one demonstration at the capitol in midwinter when it was well below zero and we were so cold we seriously hoped to be arrested just so we could go inside and get warm. No such luck.

In spite of my civil rights and antiwar activities, I hadn't entirely given up on the existing political system and still considered myself an active Democrat. This binary approach to political action has remained my style throughout my life, in the hope that one approach or the other will work. At times it has made me the brunt of jokes and sarcastic comments. But I suspect that I began to hone the ability to work with just about anyone for the end I desired as an "other" at U-High. And now, undaunted, as a freshman at Wisconsin in a presidential election year, I got quickly and heavily involved in the leadup work to UW's 1964 mock presidential election campaign, and of necessity learned how to juggle friendships with my two very different groups of friends, the mostly East Coast antiwar radicals and the mostly Midwestern establishment liberals.

The mock Minnesota delegation—of which I was a member—was leading the charge on behalf of Lyndon Johnson and Minnesota's favorite son, Hubert Humphrey. Admittedly this was a particularly odd pairing with my radical antiwar work, since Johnson and Humphrey were all about winning the war at any cost; but at that point my hope was still that we could create a groundswell of support for a U.S. exit from Vietnam that would give the president the cover he needed to get out.

In the process of working on the mock election I began spending time with the guy who was chairing the mock Minnesota delegation, a Madison native and UW sophomore, who was high up in the large and active UW Young Dems group. He knew most of the politicians around Madison as he came from a politically active family, and this gave me the opportunity to do some real-life campaign work for the first time, see what a private fundraising event looked like, and meet some real life politicians. Some days it was difficult to tell where my passion for politics ended and my passion for him began, but as both were positive involvements it didn't really matter much.

My sophomore year I applied to and was accepted into a national YM/YWCA summer program, the College Summer Service Group (CSSG), in New York City. By this time, I was deeply involved in a new romance and considered myself unofficially engaged to another Madison native from another political family. My mother was in a panic over the seriousness of the relationship, so she was only too happy to send me off to New York for the summer.

The CSSG was one of a half dozen projects developed by the national Ys to involve college students in President Lyndon Johnson's War on Poverty. The project described itself as an opportunity to live at the historic Henry Street Settlement House on New York's Lower East Side and work with inhabitants of the city's slums on any of a myriad of social problems. When my acceptance materials came in it seemed that I would live with about a dozen other college-aged men and women, and travel with two of them up to Harlem each day to my work assignment as a teacher's aide in a Head Start program run by an organization called HARYOU-ACT, short for Harlem Youth Opportunities Unlimited.

My goals in applying to the program were several. First, of course, I wanted to do something socially useful. But I also hoped to get to know others who had interests similar to mine but rooted in different backgrounds, learn about the political and social justice work they had been doing, and test out the suitability of group work to my temperament. I looked forward to a firsthand view of Harlem and the problems of its preschool-aged children. When I read about HARYOU-ACT as a politically controversial organization, my curiosity was further aroused.

It was an interesting summer to say the least. Those of us who worked in the Harlem Head Start program were the only white people we saw in the course of a typical day, which was an education in itself. No one who was present at the Head Start center seemed to be in charge or to know how things were supposed to work, which made our integration into the program somewhat rocky. The first day the children were to appear, only two showed up rather than the thirty we had expected. We were sent out into a neighborhood we didn't know to go door to door trying to find the others, with mixed results.

As the summer wore on, buses for field trips failed to materialize and supplies ran out. The supervising teachers were mostly girls younger than us, with less education than we had, and no group work experience, but who were being paid hefty salaries. When we later heard that HARYOU-ACT had wanted to make the program all-Black to the point of hiring unqualified people in an attempt to empower the community with jobs and self-respect, it was easy to believe.

It was a challenging two months, but with a ratio of four adults to fifteen children for each morning and afternoon session, quite a bit of learning took place. The children learned specific skills such as counting, naming colors, and playing games; became more socialized and familiar with a school setting; and learned to follow directions. We could have done much more in the way of field trips and perhaps more formal classroom learning—all things which had been planned but were never carried out— but the children's development despite the absence of these activities was significant, and made me a lifelong proponent of Head Start, a program that has served as a model for many other variations on the theme, and whose worth has never successfully been challenged on its merits.

The group spirit and exchange I had sought from the CSSG program was a bit of a disappointment, perhaps because, contrary to our expectations, the dozen or so of us in the project were housed in two different locations and worked in so many different agencies. The seminars we attended once a week after dinner together were more fruitful. Each of us in turn was given the opportunity to invite any speaker we wished to come to dinner and address the group, and many of the speakers were amazingly brilliant and accomplished people, like Constance Baker Motley, a pioneering Black civil rights lawyer and activist who, among other things, had drafted the complaint in *Brown vs. Board of Education*, and Ralph Abernathy, also Black, who organized both the Montgomery bus boycott and the Southern Christian Leadership Conference, a leading civil rights organization.

Spending my summer evenings having small-group discussions with unquestionably famous people was both educational and inspiring, and I believe that it was at Henry Street where my ability to question important people and my confidence in approaching just about anyone for anything really blossomed.

When it was my turn to select a speaker, I chose Norman Thomas, the perennial candidate for president on the Socialist Party ticket, whose politics I admired. The night he came we had dinner up on the roof because the temperature inside the building on this New York summer night was so oppressive. As it happened, that day the U.S. had escalated its bombing of North Vietnam, so Thomas had quite a lot to say as we sat under the stars and took in his wisdom.

All in all, it was an amazing summer. I returned home, then went off to Madison again, more convinced than ever that my role in life somehow had to involve attempting to change the world for the better. As for my faux fiancé, after he came to visit me in St. Paul and got a taste of my mother's displeasure and inhospitality, our relationship cooled; he went off to Texas and law school, and soon married someone else.

Academically, I enjoyed Wisconsin very much and did well, being elected to Crucible, the junior women's honor society, in the spring of my sophomore year. I have loved to read and learn new things as long as I can remember, and college was heaven for me. I had no specific academic or career goal in mind but found myself taking anthropology, sociology, and psychology courses along with a fair number of literature courses. Many of them were memorable, some because of the professors—such as Harry Harlow, who taught Experimental Psychology and was famous for his monkey studies and classroom imitations of primates—others for their nonacademic challenges.

Anthropology 101, a general survey course, was one of those memorable for its nonacademic challenges. By the end of the semester we had covered an enormous amount of information that we would be responsible for knowing on the final exam. Always the serious student, when our teaching assistant announced that he would offer a pre-exam study session in Vilas Park on the Saturday before the final, I leapt at the opportunity to increase my chances of doing well, riding my bike to the park with my books and notebooks stashed in my saddlebags.

I needn't have bothered to bring the books. I was the only one who came actually expecting to study the semester's material; everyone else came with a six-pack of beer and who knows what else. By the end of the afternoon I'd had as much to drink as any of them, and mounting my bicycle set off with a wobble back to Lake Lawn Hall. When I got to the corner of Park and University things came undone: I miscalculated the turn, crashed into the curb, and bike, books, and I went sprawling. I was bleeding in a few places but not seriously injured, and after picking myself up and taking a deep breath, made it the rest of the way back, arriving dirty, torn, bruised, and bleeding and with no more knowledge of anthropology than I'd left with.

As a sophomore I had enrolled in Seymour Abrahamson's Genetics course to meet my science requirement, because I had enjoyed biology in high school and had had some positive exposure to the science behind the inheritance of physical traits in my anthropology classes. Abrahamson was a recognized authority in his field and an excellent teacher. Going to class and listening to him was a real treat, until my utter lack of math and science background made it impossible for me to keep up with the material or understand what he was talking about.

I continued going to class and enjoying the lectures, but I knew I was falling further and further behind. When I was hospitalized with mononucleosis a week before the final exam and couldn't stay awake long enough to review what little I *did* know, I knew I was doomed. I did the best I could to explain my situation to Abrahamson when I was released from the hospital, and he was very understanding. I've always considered the D I got on the final exam and the C I got in the course a gift, and a nod to my continuing interest in the subject matter.

I made both freshman and sophomore honors at Wisconsin and held an academic scholarship for the two and a half years I was there, but returning from my summer in New York City and starting my junior year in the fall of 1965 I was increasingly uncertain whether I should be in college at all when I didn't seem to have an academic goal in mind. I was paying the balance of my tuition over and above my nonresident scholarship from my earnings at the Y and at the dining hall of my new dorm, but I knew that my room and board were costing my parents a lot of hard-earned money, and it didn't seem right to be spending it on an education whose direction I wasn't sure of.

My father and I discussed the issue nearly every time I came home. I would tell him that I didn't want to spend his money without knowing what I was spending it for, and he would tell me that the reason he always worked so hard to make money was so that my brother and I could have the opportunities that he hadn't had to do interesting things. That only made me feel worse.

So, when my mother came up with the idea that I should go spend some time living on an Israeli kibbutz with my aunt and her family, the idea seemed a good one, and when the first semester of my junior year ended in January, I found myself back in St. Paul preparing to go to Israel for the next six months. My aunt and her Canadian husband had moved to Israel in 1954 with a Zionist youth group just six years after Israel achieved statehood. I hadn't seen them since and they now had four children and lived at Kibbutz Urim in the Negev Desert.

*   *   *

On February 11, 1966, I set sail on the *S.S. Israel*, the one remaining passenger ship of the ZIM line, Israel's national shipping line, which was making its last voyage across the sea before it would be retired. Jane Ehrlich's mother Doris was my travel agent, and came in from Connecticut to meet my plane from the Twin Cities and get me safely to the boat. Among the items I carried with me were three dozen babies' undershirts. It seems that at the time all Israeli-made undershirts pulled over the babies' heads, and the kibbutz wanted some that snapped up the side, so I became the designated carrier. It took a bit of explaining at customs.

We were due to arrive in Haifa, Israel, on March 2. On board I took up with a lively crowd of young, sophisticated, mostly Israeli passengers for the three-week trip. One of them lived at the small kibbutz I was going to. A South African who had made *aliyah* (emigrated to Israel) after high school in late 1958, his presence on the ship gave me a small-world feeling that was reassuring out there in the middle of the Atlantic Ocean, as I wondered at times what I had gotten myself into.

I also made friends with some of the ship's crew, mainly a sailor named Eli. Because it was the ship's last cruise, things were being played pretty loose in the crew quarters, and hanging out with Eli meant seeing parts of the ship I would otherwise never have seen. One night, while dancing with members of the crew on the lower deck aft as we sailed through the Straits of Gibraltar, with lights sparkling at us from a different continent on either side, I could hardly believe that I was where I was, and that I was actually experiencing that incredible moment.

Eli was dark and handsome and just what I thought a young Israeli man should look like. It was my good fortune to have him as an escort when we docked at various ports and went ashore, since he knew the port cities well and the best places to eat. He spoke some English and I'd just finished two semesters of Hebrew at Wisconsin, having become weary of studying German, so we managed to communicate adequately. When we arrived at our destination of Haifa he promised he'd come and visit me.

I arrived in Israel without a lot of preconceived notions about what it was like. I was neither religious, nor well-schooled in Jewish history; nor was I the daughter of an ethnic home, or the product of an American Zionist youth movement. Yet I loved almost every minute of the six months I was there, responding quickly and enthusiastically to the strong sense of purpose of its inhabitants, and the feeling of community on the kibbutz.

At Urim I lived in a very primitive two-room wooden cabin, with separate entrances to each room. I shared my room with an army girl my age from Beersheva who was assigned to Urim to teach in the elementary school. The adjacent room on the other side of the wall housed the two Druze men who were the kibbutz's night guards. The degree to which those two Arab men were trusted with the lives of everyone on the kibbutz was an important lesson for me, and one I never forgot.

Once oriented, I was assigned to work in the *gan*, or kindergarten. The kids were about the same age as the children I'd worked with in Head Start. Most of them spoke no English at all, nor did some of the teachers, but I was fortunate that my aunt's kibbutz had been founded by two youth groups that had made *aliyah* at the same time and been sent to this spot in the Negev desert in 1946 to create a settlement. One group was made up of Bulgarians, but the other was made up of Americans and Canadians, so there were many adult English speakers around.

I took my job seriously but knew that I was free to come and go, and I did do a lot of traveling. There were relatives to meet in other places and so many things to see! During my six-month stay, I saw a good share of the country, from the northernmost point of Rosh Ha'Nikrah on the Lebanese border to Eilat at the Red Sea. It was a peaceful time in Israel: Travel was unrestricted, and everyone was welcoming. Jews and Arabs of many stripes mixed easily in stores and restaurants, on public transportation, and in the small towns and cities.

My aunt knew I'd studied archaeology at Wisconsin and arranged for me to spend time on a dig with one of the kibbutzniks who was an amateur archaeologist. Joe and I traveled together to Pardes Hanna, just northeast of Tel Aviv, where we bunked at the agricultural school close to Tel Zeror, a site consisting of two small tels, one containing building remains from the Canaanite period (3150-1200 BCE), and the other, remains from the Israelite period (1200-586 BCE). The tels had not yet been identified and their ancient names were unknown, but significant objects were being unearthed in both areas, focusing on a cemetery in one and a residential area in the other. I happily worked in the cemetery for a week, developing an emotional connection to this ancient community. I was allowed to keep as mementos a tooth, a bead, and several broken pieces of pottery that I unearthed, which were apparently of no special value to anyone else but were treasures to me.

Eli from the *S.S. Israel* came to visit me at the kibbutz as promised, and caused quite a stir. It turned out that his dark and handsome good looks were not what many Israelis thought a young Israeli man should look like at all, as I had, but were rather the natural physical characteristics of an Iraqi Jew, which it turned out was not who many of the kibbutzniks thought a nice American girl like me should be hanging around with. It was a brutal lesson to learn that racism was alive and well in Israel, and that it has made life difficult for the many Jewish immigrants from places like Iraq and Ethiopia, who made *aliyah* in the hope of finding their homeland, but have been disappointed in their reception and the challenge of finding good employment.

Israel's political and social warts notwithstanding, I found myself attracted to the country and very much in tune with the kibbutz way of life. Living in a community that connected its various parts—residential, agricultural, commercial, educational, and recreational spaces—by curving foot paths, with vehicles restricted to an outer perimeter road, made a lot of sense to me and seemed a tangible way to encourage the integration of the corresponding parts of one's life. Eating lunch in the communal dining hall was a special time to check in with family and friends and make plans for later in the day. Having a swimming pool, cultural center with movie theatre, library, and art gallery just a short walk from my room was also a pleasure and kept the kibbutz from feeling too much like the isolated outpost in the middle of nowhere that it was. I was sold on this degree of communal living, and vowed to finish college as quickly and simply as possible at the University of Minnesota, then return to Israel to live for the foreseeable future.

*   *   *

I sailed toward home on the Greek ship *Queen Anna Maria* on August 7. One day out of New York harbor, while partying with new friends, I received a phone call from my father informing me that he and my mother would not be able to meet my ship when it docked as they had planned, as my mother had just had surgery that day for breast cancer. They looked forward to seeing me soon, but it would be my friend Jane Ehrlich, and her mother Doris, who had arranged my trip and seen me off in February, who would meet me at the ship instead and get me on a plane headed for home.

By the time I got off the ship I was pretty much of a mess. All of the women I'd known to that point who'd had breast cancer—mostly close relatives or friends of my mother's—had died. I was terrified that I might lose my mother, anxious to get home, and had not another thought in my head about anything else. Jane and Doris were wonderfully supportive: concerned and compassionate about my mother's illness, they tried to engender hope in me and salvage some excitement and even joy at my return. However, I have no recollection of anything that transpired from the moment they greeted me at the ship until I got off the plane in the Twin Cities many hours later.

Following my mother's surgery, radiation treatment, and a course of chemotherapy, she improved and returned to work as a school social worker, her job at the time. I went back to college at the U of M, got an apartment in South Minneapolis, and commuted on a red 90cc Suzuki motorcycle between my apartment, school, my secretarial job in the office of a small machine-tool company in South Minneapolis, and my parents' house in St. Paul.

College life was a thing of the past. I attended classes, majoring in psychology with a minor in history, but took no part in campus activities. Everything went well for about a year, when it was discovered that my mother's breast cancer had metastasized. She then began a series of treatments and hospitalizations, punctuated by short periods of comparative good health, that continued unabated until her death.

Tragically, not only my mother, but Jane, and shortly after her, Doris, would all be dead from breast cancer far too soon—my mother three years later at 51, Jane at just 40 years of age, and Doris not long after burying her daughter.

Chapter Six

The McCarthy Campaign

1968

I. Minnesota

I could easily write an entire book about the events of 1968; many people have, others still are; there's no lack of material. For me the year was my defining moment, and the vehicle was politics: the campaign of Minnesota's junior U.S. Senator, Eugene J. McCarthy, for president of the United States.

I had moved back to my parents' house in mid-1967 to help out with the management of my mother's illness. I was still there in December when my father got a phone call asking us all to plan on attending our March 5 precinct caucus to support McCarthy's candidacy, and to do what we could to encourage like-minded neighbors to do the same.

In Minnesota at the time, the Democratic Farmer Labor party elected a third of its national political convention delegates from the grassroots up. In every year in which there was a presidential election, DFL members would gather at precinct or ward caucuses held in homes and schools across the state to elect delegates to county and district conventions who would later elect delegates to the state convention. Delegates from that body would then be elected to the national convention, joining others selected by another process.

But the grassroots hadn't been meaningfully organized for years. Precinct and ward caucuses typically consisted of a few party regulars getting together to elect each other. The system was ripe for a takeover.

I had become involved with a group of young people publishing a newsletter called *The MATRIX* out of a campus apartment on the West Bank of the Mississippi River. A couple of the people involved with *The MATRIX* were Vietnam veterans and the newsletter had a radically antiwar position. My work had attracted me to McCarthy's candidacy, though I didn't know much about him other than that he was against the war. But over the next year the more I learned, the more I liked and came to respect this man who had quietly and courageously put himself forward to help end the war in Vietnam and point the country in a new direction.

McCarthy's view of government was based on a limited presidency supported by an active, participatory democracy, through which people could translate their hopes for the future into political change. Never a fan of top-down power in any context, this view resonated loudly with me.

McCarthy's campaign style reflected his views. He was low key, at times to a fault, and in his speeches laid out the problems that he hoped his listeners would respond to. But he did not harangue them; it was up to them to take action or not. Richard Stout, in his book about the campaign, *People,* quotes Frederick Pohl of New Jersey, a McCarthy leader in his community:

> To me, and to most of the scores of McCarthy supporters I know well, McCarthy was almost incidental to the movement. I admire him personally, but he did not lead me, or most of the others I know in the sense he changed my views in any way. I have been involved in scores of campaigns. In all but one of them I was working for a

candidate. In the McCarthy campaign I felt that he was working for me.[9]

I felt precisely the same as Pohl did, and so by the time March came around I was proudly FMBNH, as the esoteric little white button with black letters would later declare to those in the know: For McCarthy Before New Hampshire. I'd begun volunteering at McCarthy headquarters in St. Paul, and unbeknownst to the senator, for the next eight months he was working for me, too.

Minnesota's favorite son, Hubert Humphrey, was at the time vice president of the United States under President Lyndon Johnson. The Johnson/Humphrey ticket had the support of the Democratic mainstream, and was assumed by many to be the shoo-in ticket. My father admired many of Humphrey's liberal ideas, but he, too, was strongly opposed to the Vietnam war and was old enough to remember Humphrey's high-handedness when the DFL was formed, as well as his sponsorship of the Internal Security Act of 1950, providing for detention camps for communists similar to those in which Japanese Americans had been incarcerated during World War II. Turning toward McCarthy was not a difficult move for him to make.

My father was enthusiastic about McCarthy's candidacy, but working the better part of six days a week and caring for my mother took up most of his time and energy. In the evening he spent what time he had developing a list of acquaintances who lived in our neighborhood who he thought would be likely to support McCarthy. It then became my job to contact them to convey our family's endorsement, let them know when and where their precinct caucus would be held, and ask for their support.

---

[9] Richard Stout, *People* (Harper and Row, 1970), 123-4.

I had never been to a precinct caucus, and if my father or mother had, it was before I was old enough to be aware of it. Whatever actions they might have taken as college students, and as politically interested and aware as they were, I remember them in my lifetime mainly as political intellectuals, devouring *I. F. Stone's Weekly,* the *Nation, Commentary,* and the *Progressive* as soon as they arrived in the mail.

I don't remember much about our March 5 caucus other than McCarthy's win in our precinct, my father's election as a delegate to the county convention, and the ease with which these two things had been accomplished just by making some phone calls. If anyone had told me that night that I'd be on the campaign trail myself in less than a month, and that by the time I returned to Minnesota in June for the state convention I would be a seasoned veteran of five presidential primaries and considered a valued political operative, I wouldn't have believed them. But, that's exactly what happened.

McCarthy's showing in the Minnesota precinct caucuses was very strong throughout the state. Without personally campaigning himself, but with a volunteer organization motivated by a desire to end the Vietnam war, his delegates carried all three metropolitan congressional districts by margins of up to 5 to 1. In the 4th congressional district, which included St. Paul, his delegates carried sixteen of eighteen state legislative districts. In a state long blindly in love with Hubert Humphrey, McCarthy carried every major city and upended the political establishment. Among the longtime politicians defeated that night in their local precinct caucuses were the sitting secretary of state, the mayor of St. Paul, and Hubert Humphrey's son and son-in-law.

A large group of us who had worked on behalf of McCarthy took over a neighborhood bar near headquarters that night to celebrate the victory. Many of the same people who had gathered in our basement for the Wallace fundraiser in 1948, and also some of their children, were present.

Then a senior at the University of Minnesota, though I'd hardly attended classes since I'd been volunteering at McCarthy headquarters, I felt a surge of gratitude toward my parents for the upbringing I'd had, the values they instilled in me, and our ability to work together for the same social and political ends.

My mother was very ill then but came out for the caucus and the celebration, and I took some comfort in the fact that she knew I would carry on her political tradition if she were to die not knowing anything else about what my future life would be like.

My eyes filled with tears then as they did thirty-four years later, when my daughter Elizabeth, then a senior at UW-Madison, called to report on her completion of a "Freedom Ride" course that had taken her through the South with other UW students, retracing the steps of the original civil rights activists and talking to many who had been leaders of that struggle. When she told me how grateful she was that her father and I had raised her the way we had, instilling in her a passion for social justice and a commitment to work toward its realization, I knew exactly how she felt.

*   *   *

After the precinct caucuses, I immediately increased my volunteer work for McCarthy by reporting to state headquarters on a daily basis. In a manner I would come to know as characteristic of the campaign nationally, simply by virtue of my willingness to show up every day, put in many hours of hard work, and not be afraid to step up and take responsibility when some task needed doing, in less than a week I was given the title of coordinator of Minnesota volunteers. My job was recruiting, training, and deploying groups of Minnesotans—largely but by no means exclusively college students—to door-to-door canvassing locations in Wisconsin, where McCarthy was on the ballot in the April 2 Democratic primary.

Adults more than twice my age—including many prominent political and community leaders—accepted my rise to a leadership position without question. They dealt with me as an equal and took it for granted that I knew what I was doing. Remarkably, though I'd done nothing of the sort before, it never occurred to me either that I didn't. The fact is, political organizing isn't complicated. The volunteer coordinator job, like every political organizing job I would take on for the rest of my life, called not for specialized knowledge, but rather personal traits and skills that my parents, teachers, and other adults I'd known had been modeling for me for years, or that I'd had a chance to hone elsewhere. I found I could combine these into an approach that inspired other people and helped me lead by example. I worked long hours and I worked intensely. I delegated responsibility freely, but carefully. I knew what I believed in, and devoted myself to attaining it.

Campaign work is interesting in the way it forces you to define what's a reasonable amount of work to get done in a given amount of time. In the space of a week, sometimes a day or less, plans must be made and executed, actions shaped, reshaped, then taken, sometimes affecting thousands if not hundreds of thousands of people. This is true whether the campaign is for a candidate or a cause. It is life lived at top speed, and is an environment in which a good organizer excels: You see a need, then you do what's needed. It requires good sense, self-confidence in your decision making, and total commitment to the candidate or cause.

Campaign work is not an environment suited to everyone, and many people fear it. But it came naturally to me, and has always been an environment in which I am comfortable. For this I credit my childhood, which developed my fearlessness, my early education, which taught me what I was capable of, and my high school years, which developed the resilience I needed to continue on after failure and disappointment.

Later in life, when I would work with nonprofit boards on the seemingly endless tasks of developing mission statements or long-term strategic goals, it would test my patience and sometimes require every ounce of restraint I had to curb my urge to act rather than plan. But as soon as I joined the McCarthy campaign, I felt like a horse just let out of the barn and given its head. I felt that my entire life to that point had prepared me for this challenge. I was comfortable in the public eye, confident of my judgment and ability to make quick, solid decisions, and yes, essentially fearless in this arena.

II. Wisconsin

Our task at McCarthy headquarters from the day after Minnesota's precinct caucuses to the day of the April 2 Wisconsin primary was to support the Wisconsin McCarthy campaign by sending door-to-door canvassers into Wisconsin's 3rd and 10th congressional districts, in the northwest quadrant of the state. For the first several weeks canvassers focused on educating voters on the senator's positions and taking their political temperatures; then, on the weekend before the primary and especially on election day, everything we did was focused on turning out the favorable vote.

When McCarthy received 42 percent of the vote in New Hampshire's first-in-the-nation Democratic primary on March 12, and the entire country woke up to the fact that President Lyndon Johnson had lost the support of the American people for his Vietnam war policy, calls began to pour into headquarters: How can I help in Wisconsin? Where can I go to canvass? What exactly do I do when I get there? Because Wisconsin's largest population centers were either on the other side of the state in Milwaukee—its largest city—or in the southern part of the state in Madison—its capital—in our location in the Twin Cities, perched just thirty-five miles from Wisconsin's northwestern border, our volunteers were critical to covering the state's northwestern tier.

Door-to-door canvassing is in and of itself a very simple task. For an election, it involves knocking on a stranger's door, introducing yourself, stating on whose behalf you have come, and engaging the stranger in a brief conversation about your candidate's position on the issues the person cares about. If no one is home, which is often the case on weekends when many working people run their errands, the canvasser generally leaves a piece of literature with a brief, prewritten note and moves on.

Given the number of doors a canvasser is typically asked to knock on in a morning or afternoon, there isn't time for lengthy conversation. And, most canvassers don't have the in-depth knowledge of their candidate's positions on a wide enough range of issues to support that kind of engagement, even if there were time.

Usually the goal of the conversation from the canvasser's point of view is to determine what issues the voter cares about, offer them a persuasive reason to support the candidate if they're undecided, and then rate the likelihood that the voter will do so on election day. When election day comes, other volunteers will take that information and make sure that favorable voters get to the polls.

Canvassers for McCarthy were of many types: longtime activists, mothers with children in tow, and of course college students—all strongly opposed to the war. It was surely not the first campaign to utilize a door-to-door canvass, but it was by far the most extensive nationwide canvassing operation anyone could remember, and unique in the extent to which volunteer canvassers dropped out of school, quit jobs, and otherwise temporarily abandoned their ordinary lives to take part in it.

Inspired by newspaper and television stories of how their counterparts in New Hampshire had turned that primary election upside down in McCarthy's favor, canvassers who went into Wisconsin were anxious to do it again there. First-time volunteers feared the worst: that people would scream and shout at them, that doors would be slammed in their face, that dogs would rise up to attack them, or that they would be found out to be mere ordinary citizens who didn't have all the answers to the great problems of the day.

All of these things do happen, but rarely. I have found over the years that canvassing is almost always a pleasant experience, and one's status as an ordinary person without all the answers a plus. This was certainly true with the McCarthy campaign in state after state. Americans were tired of the war in Vietnam and the toll it was taking in human lives. They were looking for a way out of it. Gene McCarthy was an unknown figure to most of them; they were curious to know more about him, and if he could really help achieve that objective.

Wisconsin voters were equally curious about the canvassers who appeared at their door: who they were, where they came from, and why they cared about Gene McCarthy's candidacy so much that they had uprooted themselves to campaign. Far from feeling like they had been invaded by foreigners with questionable motives, the people canvassed were pleased that their thoughts were considered valuable, that we cared how they felt about the issues and why, and that we had come such distances to take the time and trouble to come to their door and inquire. In most cases no one had ever done that before, and that was undeniably a part of the campaign's magic. Today, when so many people have become alienated from their government, door-to-door canvassing has again become a critical tool for restoring to voters a feeling that they can and do have a personal say in the major policy decisions of our time, and for reminding them that that's what democracy is all about.

There were four weekends between the Minnesota precinct caucuses and the Wisconsin primary. After New Hampshire it was not so much a question of recruiting canvassers willing to go to Wisconsin and help, as it was of utilizing them effectively. For us in the St. Paul headquarters that meant providing a short but thorough and reassuring orientation complete with hot coffee and snacks, making sure they each had their own packet of literature to review on the way to their canvassing location so they could answer basic questions about McCarthy's positions, getting them assigned and loaded into the right cars and buses in the right numbers, and getting those cars and buses deployed in a timely fashion to the Wisconsin towns and cities where they were needed.

McCarthy's national staff in Milwaukee determined the canvassing locations in advance. Even in this precomputer age it seemed as if demographic data and previous voting patterns were endlessly being crunched and analyzed. Our main contact was Bobbie Kramer, who introduced herself over the phone as a Wellesley College student taking a leave of absence to work on the campaign. When she was unavailable we dealt with the equally efficient Belle Huang or Susan Spear. They told us where our canvassers were needed and in what numbers, and we took it from there.

Some Minnesota colleges organized canvassers by the busload. These buses were then deployed by our office to towns in Wisconsin that were sizable or organized enough to have asked for a large number of canvassers who could cover the entire town in a single day. When the volunteers arrived they were met by local McCarthy people who had divided the town into walking routes and ferried them to the neighborhoods they needed to cover, and then turned them loose. After a few hours they would pick them up again, collect the information they had obtained, and make sure everyone got back on the bus to go home.

In 1968 much of the work associated with a well-organized canvassing operation was still being done by hand and without access to much detailed voter information. In rural areas it was not uncommon not even to know the name of the person on whose door you were knocking, let alone anything else about them. Today, with the ability to import helpful information from larger and more detailed databases, canvassers generally know the name, age, and gender of whomever they're going to be talking to; whether they're a Democrat, Republican, or unaffiliated voter; which of the last several elections they've voted in; and often more.

Regardless of how much information canvassers have about a voter before beginning a conversation, the single most important task when they end it is always rating the voter. Usually this is a 1, 2, 3, 4, or 5, indicating how likely the voter is to vote for the candidate. Those ratings then guide the crucial election day get-out-the-vote activities to make sure that every favorable voter actually votes. That means a phone call and a gentle reminder of how very important their vote really is, and depending on the voter's response that call might lead to a ride to the polls, or providing child care while they vote.

On Saturday and Sunday mornings our headquarters looked like a relocation center. Volunteers were given strict instructions to arrive by 8:30 am Saturday or 10:30 am Sunday for instructions, with departure for points in Wisconsin scheduled for 9:00 and 11:00 sharp on those respective days.

Canvassers were also told how to dress. Rigid standards of dress and appearance were imposed on all canvassers, and "Clean for Gene" became a mantra for the campaign. There was plenty of behind-the-scenes work to be done by volunteers who didn't care to conform to the conservative standards of rural Wisconsin, but they wouldn't be sent out of our office as visible supporters of the senator.

In an interview with the *Minneapolis Star,* I said that it was critical to make a good first impression. For many of the people we'd be meeting, this would be their first direct contact with the political process and perhaps their only contact with a representative of McCarthy. As volunteer coordinator I took very seriously our responsibility to make that first impression a favorable one. We made no exceptions.

On March 16, I hurried back from the day's canvassing operation to receive my Bachelor of Arts degree, magna cum laude with honors in psychology, at the University of Minnesota's winter commencement. It was an important day in my life and a proud one for my parents, who attended the ceremony in Northrup Memorial Auditorium along with thousands of other beaming parents.

But by then I was living and breathing the McCarthy campaign, and my enjoyment of the event was overshadowed by Senator Robert F. Kennedy's announcement earlier that day that he would also be an antiwar candidate for president.

No one could predict at that point exactly what effect Kennedy's announcement would have on the McCarthy campaign, but all of us knew that it wouldn't be good. At a minimum, the two candidates would split the antiwar vote, as well as the money and energy needed to turn it out.

Much has been written about the timing and wisdom of Bobby Kennedy's entry into the Democratic primary race. His challenge to McCarthy's antiwar candidacy, after McCarthy had stepped forward and put himself on the line to prove that opposition to the war was a politically viable platform, was very controversial.

Ideologically, I didn't dislike Bobby Kennedy. I agreed with his positions on most issues. As a campaign opponent, however, I thought he had used McCarthy badly, and it seemed that in state after state, incident after incident, his campaign workers were needlessly aggressive toward ours on a personal level.

But most of all, philosophically, I didn't like Kennedy's approach to racial minorities and other groups traditionally underrepresented in the political process. I developed a strong visual image of what this approach looked like: a patchwork quilt. And it seemed to me that, like a patchwork quilt, as soon as any real stress was applied it would fall apart at the seams.

McCarthy had a more blended approach. He readily acknowledged the special problems and issues that different groups of people faced, but preferred to address them holistically, as resulting from the same failure of government to protect the basic rights and liberties shared by all Americans, no matter the color of their skin, their sex, their religion, or anything else. This made eminently more sense to me at a very basic level, and remains my position to this day.

Kennedy's declaration of candidacy came too late for him to get on the ballot in Wisconsin, so going into the last half of March we remained happily awash in volunteers. A big push was not only to line up canvassers for the last weekend of door-to-door work before the primary, but also to get commitments from volunteers to canvass during the entire week before election day, and to work on election day itself making reminder phone calls, poll watching, providing rides and child care, and doing "honk and waves" at busy intersections. By the last week of March, we were sending canvassers out of our office every morning and welcoming them back tired but fulfilled at the end of a long day.

As part of the final push I was asked to help student government leaders at the University of Minnesota publicize a volunteer recruitment rally slated for Northrup Memorial Auditorium on campus March 27. The program would be headlined by popular actor Paul Newman, and by Allard Lowenstein, one of the founders of the "Dump Johnson" movement; both had been working tirelessly for McCarthy since New Hampshire and would continue to do so for the duration of the campaign.

Together with my friend and campaign colleague Tom Barrett, I rushed to close up the St. Paul headquarters the evening before the rally once the calls had subsided and the office had been prepared for the next day. Armed with plenty of tape, thumb tacks and flyers advertising the rally, we drove over to the U and went into distribution mode in the dark. Having attended classes, plays, concerts, banquets, graduations, athletic events, and political rallies on campus for 13 years, I knew where we needed to go. Blanketing both the East and West Bank campuses, as well as the pedestrian level of the bridge across the Mississippi River that connects them, we hit bulletin boards inside and out, and also the walls of dormitories, classroom buildings, student centers, libraries, and cafeterias. It was midnight when we finished, and I don't think we missed many good spots.

The crowd of 6,000 people that assembled at Northrop Auditorium the next morning was the largest crowd ever assembled in the building for a single program. Fire marshals demanded clear aisles, but even after two delays to accomplish this, students, faculty, and staff were still standing, sitting, and kneeling in every inch of space. Newman urged the students to go to Wisconsin that last weekend to work for McCarthy. "It's a big feeling, a big feeling," he said, "and you'll be a better person for having been part of it."[10] He received a standing ovation when he finished.

Meanwhile, I had received a call earlier that day from Sandy Silverman at McCarthy headquarters in Milwaukee. Silverman introduced herself as Newman's scheduler, and said she had called to alert me to some logistical challenges that had cropped up in regard to his appearance in Minneapolis. Originally he had planned to fly from Wisconsin to Minneapolis in a private plane, then barnstorm his way back to Milwaukee, stopping off for smaller rallies at towns along the way. However, it being March in Minnesota, bad weather had fouled up the plan. He instead had to take a commercial flight that would get him to the rally more or less on time, but which would leave him without a way to meet the rest of the day's schedule.

"Could you provide a driver as far as Eau Claire?" Silverman asked. If we could manage that first leg of the trip—a matter of 95 miles one way— others were prepared to take over from there.

Was she kidding? Spend a couple of hours driving around with Paul Newman? I was, after all, a twenty-two-year-old young woman. This was clearly an opportunity not to be missed! We were up to our ears already

---

[10] *Minnesota Daily,* March 28, 1968, 1.

handling a daily flood of phone calls that we knew would increase exponentially after the rally, but with experienced volunteers who could do the drill in their sleep by now, I said that Tom and I would be happy to personally make sure that Newman got where he needed to go.

We left directly after the rally, Tom driving us in his car. As directed by Silverman we had a salami sandwich and a six-pack of Budweiser waiting when Newman got in, and he grinned as he spotted the provisions. "I see you got all the important instructions," he said, as he voraciously launched into the sandwich.

We had just made it over the border into St. Paul when Newman got mustard on the front of his shirt, and asked that we stop somewhere so he could buy a new one. This was Tom's area of expertise, not mine, and fortunately we were in an area he knew well. He pulled into a small strip mall with a men's clothing store and Newman went in and bought himself a replacement shirt. A couple of beers later he fell asleep and we drove on uneventfully to Eau Claire.

It was raining steadily when we reached Eau Claire. Nonetheless, there in Owen Park, a large and enthusiastic crowd was waiting in the pouring rain. So excited were the girls in the crowd to see and touch Newman that, as we guided him to the stage an outstretched finger slipped into my hoop earring and ripped it out of my ear. The rest was a blur. Tom and I checked in with the Eau Claire headquarters people, handed off responsibility for Newman, and headed back to the St. Paul headquarters to face the pre-weekend rush.

We were not disappointed. Of fifteen hundred volunteers sent into western Wisconsin that last weekend before the primary, twelve hundred were sent out of our office. The campaign staff in Milwaukee reached a point where they had exhausted their databases and were calling their local committees to find places to send our volunteers.

Having completed the prepared walking lists in the priority towns of Eau Claire, Marshfield, Superior, Blue Lake, Wausau, and their surrounding communities, groups on their own initiative traveled farther afield to fourteen additional cities and towns where they canvassed door to door without lists, leafletted shopping centers, and stood at intersections with signs and banners supporting McCarthy's candidacy.

We were pleased when Mike Burlingame of the national campaign staff, a Johns Hopkins graduate student working out of the Wausau headquarters, was quoted in the *Minnesota Daily* saying, "[v]olunteers from Minnesota may have 'made the difference' in Wisconsin last weekend. We were able to conduct a canvass unprecedented in its thoroughness."[11]

As for me, who so often had not been able to reach the very top of the heap in an endeavor I cared about, I was coming to realize that political organizing was something I did very well; in fact, as well as anyone I knew. It was a life-changing realization, and I felt great personal satisfaction about what we had accomplished.

Then, on Sunday evening, March 31, two days before the Wisconsin primary, President Lyndon Johnson stunned the nation by announcing that he would not be a candidate for reelection. I was in northern Wisconsin heading home after a day of making arrangements for the last two days of canvassing and election day get-out-the-vote support when I heard the news on my car radio. I immediately pulled over and listened to the entire story, hanging on every word.

Our goal had been to pressure President Johnson into getting out of Vietnam and we had done more than that: We had dumped him! I drove the rest of the way back in excitement, wondering what would happen next, and knowing that the importance of the Wisconsin primary had just exploded.

---

[11] *Minnesota Daily*, April 2, 1968, 1.

At the invitation of the national campaign staff in Milwaukee, whom we knew only as voices on the phone, Tom and I traveled to Milwaukee on Tuesday to await the results. The returns were encouraging from the start and it was a festive evening. When in the end McCarthy garnered 56 percent of the vote, having forced Johnson out of the contest and out-polled Richard Nixon, the exhausted campaign workers all broke loose—laughing, dancing, and hugging whoever was near.

The following morning the entire Wisconsin campaign organization and all remaining paid national staff assembled in the ballroom of the Wisconsin Hotel. Establishing a pattern that would repeat itself in each state the morning after its primary, a discussion of what had worked well and what needed to be improved was followed by an update on the operational plans for the remaining states, and a sorting out of the workforce. Volunteers who had proven their worth were invited to continue on as paid staff at $5/day plus travel expenses; those who were returning home said goodbye.

I was invited to join the national staff and accepted immediately. I had found my calling and wasn't about to lose it. I was told to report to Indianapolis on April 7 to begin campaigning for the May 7 primary there, which gave me the next four days off. These would prove to be my only days off until after the Democratic National Convention in August, and they couldn't have been better timed. Two days later, Dr. Martin Luther King Jr. was shot and killed in Memphis, and I was glad to be at home, exactly where I needed to be to work through my shock and grief together with my parents.

III. Indiana and Nebraska

I left St. Paul for Indianapolis with my parents' blessing. My mother was not in good shape at all, but she and my father had fallen into a routine of sorts for her to get to necessary medical appointments with the help of friends, and as I had already been working more than full time on the campaign, my departure wasn't going to necessitate a change in anything. My mother especially was very happy that I seemed at last to have a purpose in life.

My experience with the campaign in Indiana, however, was a little rough at the start. For one thing, I found the headquarters in Indianapolis at the Claypool Hotel very oppressive. The hotel had suffered a major fire a year before and only part of its commercial space was in use. It felt very large and deserted, and voices and footsteps echoed in surroundings unforgivingly cold and unwelcoming. A lot of other people felt the same way about it, and we began referring to the place as the Cesspool Hotel. No doubt it was cheap and that was why we were there; but having formed close relationships in St. Paul with people working on top of each other and of necessity trained to do everyone else's task as well as their own, I disliked the abundant space that isolated campaign "departments" in different rooms.

The fact that we were assigned to sleep in a rather dirty, if not downright seedy budget hotel, The Antlers, soon dubbed the "Ant Hill" by those of us who had to live there, didn't help matters. I didn't like going home at night to bare walls, an iron bed, and uncomfortable surroundings. Being new to the national staff, I knew few of my coworkers, so going back to the hotel meant going back to my thin-walled room and listening to bunches of young people on either side of me having a good time. I have never been very good at making introductory conversation and have always avoided situations where I would have to engage in it. I felt very alone the first few nights and went to sleep eager for the next day to come, when I hoped others would notice my hard work and introduce themselves to me.

I quickly sensed that the campaign was having problems in Indiana but I wasn't close enough to the inner circle to know the details. Some things were obvious, like the fact that we weren't getting paid. Something was fouled up with the campaign's finances in Washington, but we were promised that back pay would be forthcoming once it got straightened out, and the promise was kept.

Fortunately, I soon made some good friends in Indiana who kept my spirits up. One was Mark Siegel, a young New York City politico who had taken leave from his studies at Columbia University School of Law to work as the election day coordinator for the primary states. Mark had a wonderfully dour sense of humor that could cheer me up no matter how down I was, and for that reason he's the only person I've ever allowed to call me anything remotely like his nickname for me, "Little Dinah."

Through Mark I met the equally humorous David Wilson, in his other life an English major at Bard College, who had joined the campaign in Wisconsin and been quickly promoted to field staff comptroller. Wilson proved a constant and loyal advocate for all of us with whoever it was in Washington that held the purse strings. Nearly thirty years later, when he had become Vermont's secretary of administration and I was a lobbyist for low-income Vermonters, David would again provide me with what I needed at a critical moment: a piece of financial information buried in the depths of the state budget that enabled me to successfully lobby the legislature to increase General Assitance payments to poor Vermonters by showing them exactly where they could find the money.

David Mixner had come to the campaign as a fervent opponent of the war in Vietnam. His later work as a political strategist and national gay rights advocate would take him to the highest of levels on the national stage with the election of his friend Bill Clinton, but in the short-lived intense world of the 1968 McCarthy campaign he was just a guy whose deep, rich laugh and sense of humor were always a welcome relief from the battles of the day in whatever state he showed up in.

If you detect a theme here, my need to have people around me who have a sense of humor, you are correct. I am admittedly a very serious person, sometimes too serious. My husband attributes this to being from

Minnesota, and for years has explained me to people by telling the story of vice presidential candidate Estes Kefauver, who, in 1956, when asked why he and Adlai Stevenson had failed to carry the state replied, "Have you ever tried to tell a joke in Minneapolis?" But I love a good laugh as much as anyone, and need to have them just as frequently, so I have always been drawn to others who can bring out humor in me.

After what now seems like weeks in Indianapolis, but was really only a single week, Bobbie Kramer and I were asked to go to Evansville, located in the southwest corner of Indiana near the Kentucky border, to help expand the campaign in that rural, conservative part of the state. Arriving there, I was surprised to learn that I was now in the South. My previous contacts with Indiana had been limited to its northern tier, mostly just from crossing it on car trips with my family, but I quickly learned that the Mason-Dixon line that runs through the middle of downtown Indianapolis is no joke—southern Indiana really *is* the South, and Evansville felt and sounded very foreign.

The task given to Bobbie and me was to figure out how to approach the rural population around Evansville in a way that would raise their awareness of McCarthy's campaign and platform before the May 7 primary. What we came up with was "Gene's Machine."

"Gene's Machine" was a rented cargo van, decorated on the outside with a large McCarthy banner and all sizes of what were called "ricky ticky stickers"—vinyl stickers shaped like a daisy flower, with white petals and a blue center across which was written "McCARTHY." We loaded the van with buttons, bumper stickers, brochures, and position papers, as well as our own personal possessions, and took it on the road, where it proved a very effective campaign tool.

Driving Gene's Machine around southwestern Indiana through all the small towns and hamlets would have been all we had to do to raise people's awareness of the campaign, but we did much more. Scanning local papers at night for mention of events the next day likely to draw crowds, we developed a routine where we would drive to the event, park in a prominent location, throw open the double doors on which were taped large pictures of Gene McCarthy, set up a card table in front of the doors with our literature and campaign paraphernalia, and upon donning our floppy blue-and-white McCarthy hats, start reaching out to people. Thus disguised, I had no trouble introducing myself to strangers who happened by, or convincing them that they really should take the brochure I offered and read it when they got home.

It was while traveling with Gene's Machine that I first realized the political advantage of being a reasonably attractive young woman. No one thought of us as political operatives, nor a threat to local morals or conservative values. Despite the highly responsible positions Bobbie and I had both held in the Wisconsin primary campaign, I think in Indiana we were seen by the public more as cheerleaders, and it was very effective. I've remembered the lesson many times since then while deciding on tactics: It takes different strokes for different folks.

Gene's Machine was a novelty and a conversation piece, and we were easily able to engage people in conversation. We had a large rural area to cover and no lack of places to go. We garnered quite a bit of press in the state, always with a picture, compounding our reach and effectiveness.

After a couple of nonstop weeks of Gene's Machine, however, the constant traveling, living out of a suitcase, and spending each night in the home of a different McCarthy supporter began to wear on us, especially Bobbie. She'd been on the campaign trail since New Hampshire, and decided to return to Wellesley to complete her studies and graduate.

For my part, I was equally happy when I was asked to hand over our Evansville-based Gene's Machine to new volunteers, and head to Nebraska to set up an entire fleet of Gene's Machines to operate in that state's rural areas until the May 14 primary there. Alas, to no avail. In their first two matchups McCarthy lost both Indiana and Nebraska to Bobby Kennedy by substantial margins.

IV. Oregon

The day after the Nebraska primary, the staff gathered at headquarters as usual, but it was a very different scene than the previous gathering I'd attended in Milwaukee.

Overnight, McCarthy had become the candidate who had to come from behind, and wins in the Oregon and California primaries, looming large on May 28 and June 4, respectively, were seen as crucial to his continued candidacy. With antiwar donors now splitting their financial support between McCarthy and Kennedy, money was tight just when we most needed it. The field staff was being cut in half, and of the nearly 300 of us left in Nebraska, only 127 were to board the chartered plane for Los Angeles, where half would get off and the rest would continue on to Portland. Those being dismissed were thanked for their hard work and given bus fare home. Those of us continuing on gathered up our personal belongings and headed for the airport.[12]

I was assigned to Oregon. A strong and well-functioning state organization there had the canvassing operation well in hand for a successful get-out-the-vote campaign; but state coordinators felt that impressing undecided voters with the widespread support for McCarthy was crucial to a win. That meant organizing big public events, as many as we could schedule, with celebrity speakers at every one. These events would culminate in a full day's visit to the state by McCarthy himself on May 25, three days before the vote, for which the crowds at each stop needed to be historically large.

---

[12] Ben Stavis, *We Were the Campaign: New Hampshire to Chicago for McCarthy* (Beacon Press, 1969), 92-93.

I was sent to Salem immediately upon arrival. My assignment was to introduce myself to the local committee people, establish my credentials, and then get to work organizing events and crowd building. I assumed I had been selected for this task based on my recruitment and crowd-building work in Minnesota, and for our success at attracting crowds to our Gene's Machines in Indiana and Nebraska.

I also had become known as someone who worked easily with state and local committee people without my ego or my title of "national staff" getting in the way. This would assure that my energy and whatever talent I had to offer would be well utilized, rather than rejected out of hand with suspicion or resentment. I was also known within the campaign by then as a tireless worker, willing to do whatever was necessary to get the job done. And this job was going to take some doing.

The ten days I spent in Salem are a complete blur. I was now part of a national crowd-building team formed by and under the direction of Steve Cohen, and I think it was Cohen who briefed me when I landed in Oregon; but whoever it was departed soon thereafter, and I was on my own once I got to Salem.

My week was all about arrangements and coordination—with police, city officials, other dignitaries, local committee people, shopkeepers, volunteers, and field staff at other planned stops—and above all, about publicity: designing and printing posters and leaflets, blanketing the city with them, writing press releases, and talking to radio and TV hosts and newspaper reporters.

The big day came and all went as planned. McCarthy drew large and enthusiastic crowds at every stop he made and we were cautiously optimistic about how the election would turn out. I joined the senator's entourage when it got to Salem, and flew off with him on his campaign plane when he left at the end of the day. As the plane lifted up, I felt a strong surge of accomplishment and yes, importance. I was on Gene McCarthy's chartered plane. I knew I had done a good job and I was thrilled to be a part of this effort, whose people I so admired for both their politics and their commitment, from the candidate on down to the newest volunteer.

Three days later Oregon handed Robert Kennedy the first defeat of the Kennedy family's political life, voting 44.7 percent for McCarthy to 38.8 percent for Kennedy. McCarthy was undeniably back in the game.

V. Oklahoma

We landed in Los Angeles but by the next day I was in Oklahoma City, having dinner with my Oklahoma hosts, she the coordinator of the state campaign, which had requested our help.

Oklahoma was not a primary state. Instead, its delegates to the national convention were selected by a variety of processes similar to Minnesota's system. Some had already been selected by the time I arrived in the state. The remainder would be chosen at the state convention June 29.

Although McCarthy had succeeded in establishing himself as a viable presidential candidate with his primary win in Oregon, it became clear that we now had to shift the focus of our work to influencing the large number of national convention delegates who had already been chosen or would be chosen by state party conventions over the summer. These non-primary state delegates—most of whom were party regulars and many of whom had been selected as much as two years earlier—would account for three-quarters of the total number of delegates who would choose the party's nominee for president in Chicago in August.

Mark Siegel and I were assigned to Oklahoma to support the state campaign's effort to convince its party regulars that McCarthy could win in November and go on to get us out of Vietnam. As a fallback position we hoped the delegates would remain uncommitted through the first ballot of the nominating process in Chicago, after which the favorite sons (and they *were* all sons) and the minor candidates would fall away, and the business of nominating a serious candidate would begin.

As part of our job we were also to gather intelligence on the issues important to the Oklahoma delegates, as well as on their loyalties and resentments. Influential people in our own campaign would use this information to McCarthy's advantage in Chicago, when deals needed to be made.

After six days in Oklahoma City meeting the rest of the local campaign team and arming myself with lists of national convention delegates from around the state who had already been chosen, I headed north to Enid, where I checked into a modest motel and began making calls to local McCarthy supporters, seeking their help in setting up meetings with local delegates. Mark went in the opposite direction and checked into a motel in Muskogee to do the same.

And that's where we were, in our respective motels, on the phone with each other with our respective television sets on, when Bobby Kennedy was shot before our eyes on election night in California, stunning us both and all of America with another horrifying assassination.

Mark headed for the airport and Los Angeles to be part of the top-level staff meetings; I went back to Oklahoma City to wait and see what would happen next. Clearly Kennedy's death was going to throw all previously crafted plans and strategies to the winds, but everyone was in such a state of shock that it was hard to imagine much clear thinking going on.

The next few weeks were profoundly sad ones for the country and confusing ones for the campaign. McCarthy immediately declared a moratorium on campaigning out of respect for Bobby Kennedy, and many of the 300+ staff and additional hundreds of volunteers just simply headed home from Los Angeles or wherever they happened to be.

It was no secret that at the higher levels of the campaign there was considerable disagreement over what the nature of the summer campaign should be. Rumors of decisions made and unmade were rampant. During this fraught time I went home to Minnesota to see my parents and to help with operations at the DFL state convention on June 22.

I was asked to return to Oklahoma for the last delegate push there before the state convention June 29. Despite summer delegate work having been officially suspended, some non-primary states, including Oklahoma, still wanted our help. National field staff chairman Curtis Gans still had sufficient funds to support a small field operation, so following the state convention I remained in Oklahoma and resumed my delegate work. Eventually the various factions of the campaign worked out a compromise, and a total of fifty of us ended up doing delegate work all summer.

I turned out to be surprisingly effective at intelligence gathering. As had been the case with the usually guarded and conservative Indiana voters, the Oklahoma county chairmen and their associates who were now national convention delegates just found it beyond belief that a 22-year-old girl from St. Paul was anything to fear, or even be cautious about, in the political arena. They spoke openly and honestly to me about their loyalties and adversaries, and entertained me with stories and anecdotes that provided me with considerable information about other delegates.

It almost seemed like the more important a political "boss" the person was, the less he felt he had anything to worry about from me. I turned around and passed on the intelligence I gathered to Genie [Grohman] Gans, who was coordinating the summer delegate work out of the Washington office, and to whom I reported. She was pleased with what I was giving her from Oklahoma, and because of that sent me to Texas for a short period of time right before that state's convention, to see what I could come up with from talking to delegates there.

My work in Oklahoma, however, came to an abrupt and surprising end. One evening in late July, while in Oklahoma City, I suddenly began to feel quite ill with intense abdominal pain, nausea, vomiting, and diarrhea.

Fortunately, the state McCarthy chairman, Ben Heller, himself a former Minnesotan, was a doctor and professor of medicine at Oklahoma University. In no time I was at the OU Medical Center being prepped for an emergency appendectomy, and remained there for the next four days. My mother headed down on the train with a dear family friend for company and assistance. Satisfied that I was in good hands, they returned to the Twin Cities to await my arrival when I was deemed able to travel. Peter was dispatched from Chicago, where he was then living, to bring me home.

VI. Chicago

After several more weeks of recuperation, my doctors agreed that I could go to the Democratic National Convention in Chicago if I promised to continue to rest while I was there and not jeopardize my recovery with too much activity.

I arrived in Chicago on Monday of convention week, gratified to find that the campaign organization had arranged for me to room with Mary Beth McCarthy, the senator's niece, a fellow Minnesotan who had dropped out of the University of Colorado to campaign for her uncle. Our paths hadn't previously crossed, but I was happy to be on the 23rd floor of the Hilton Hotel, where I could watch all of the convention proceedings on television; and I couldn't have asked for a better view of Grant Park across the street, where antiwar rallies and demonstrations were already going on day and night when I arrived in town.

Because the 23rd floor housed the senator and his family and close friends, I was given the highest level of convention credentials available so I could come and go through the tight security set up for their protection. The campaign staff was housed primarily on the 15th floor, where work was going on nonstop twenty-four hours a day. My credentials, I was told, also gave me access to McCarthy's operations center at the Chicago Amphitheatre, where the convention was to be held. I knew that would be a frantic place well beyond doctors' orders, however, and that I wouldn't be going there.

Late Tuesday night Mary Beth came back to the room briefly and reported that the demonstrations had ramped up a notch, with clashes with police being reported throughout the neighborhood surrounding the Hilton. Out our window Mary Travers and Peter Yarrow of Peter, Paul & Mary fame were leading songs in Grant Park. Some 4,000 people had assembled there, mainly McCarthy supporters who could not get into the convention and had nowhere else to go. The group was growing quickly and had been ringed by helmeted Chicago police. I longed to go, but dutifully held back. I knew myself well enough to know that once I left the hotel and got involved in the protests, I was not likely to return to safety.

Things came to a head on Wednesday. The peace plank proposed by the antiwar delegates went down to defeat in the afternoon, and the doomed nomination process for president began in early evening. The Grant Park crowd had been told they could march to the Amphitheatre, but when they tried to assemble they were surrounded by police in riot gear. The rest is history.

As darkness fell the police tightened their circle around the group and closed in on the peaceful crowd. Many were beaten and tear gassed, and as they tried to disperse were forced against the plate-glass wall of the Hilton's Haymarket Lounge until the glass broke. Many were badly slashed as the storm troopers stepped on and over them chasing others into the hotel lobby. The injured who could be rescued were brought up to a makeshift hospital on the 15th floor, where Senator McCarthy and two physicians in his party, including Mary Beth's father, treated their wounds.

As I watched things unfold from my hotel window the phone rang. Someone on the 15th floor had just realized that of all the staff people holding credentials sufficient to get into the Amphitheatre, I was the only one still at the hotel. Could I possibly get there and let them know what was going on in the streets and that help was needed? No one was able to get through by phone.

Communication with the Amphitheatre had been difficult since McCarthy's staff had arrived in Chicago. We attributed the problems to Chicago Mayor Richard J. Daley, a strong supporter of Hubert Humphrey and a determined opponent of Gene McCarthy's and of the antiwar protesters whom he felt had invaded his city. As the politics got increasingly tense in the Amphitheatre leading up to the nominating process, it appeared that the mayor was personally ordering the people in control of the microphones to cut off any McCarthy supporters who tried to make statements critical of the nominating process. It was suspected that he was also behind the problems with the phone lines.

Of course I agreed to go and quickly made my departure, not realizing that the distance involved was a matter of miles. I was quite frightened when I started out. The last place I wanted to be at that moment was alone in the streets of Chicago, unable to run if I needed to. But as I made my way through the streets past people sitting or lying on the ground, battered, bruised, and wounded, being comforted or cared for by complete strangers who were fortunate enough to be in better shape, it was difficult to restrain myself and I ended up doing an odd step that combined something like walking and hopping and which I hoped would not unduly stress my recently cut and stitched abdomen. I finally reached the Amphitheatre and easily gained entrance with my credentials.

I located the McCarthy operations center just as a frantic message came through from someone at the teletype on the 15th floor with a plea for help. I filled in the details and while the nominating speeches for Hubert Humphrey droned on in the background, the McCarthy staff fanned out to let our supporters on the floor know what was happening in front of the Hilton.

I was sent up into the gallery to inform our VIPs, and I remember hearing the band playing "Happy Days Are Here Again" as Humphrey's nominating speeches ended. I made my way back to the floor in a daze, turned toward the exit, and walked slowly back to the Hilton, tears streaming down my face.

I have no precise recollection of what I did or didn't do after my trip to the Amphitheatre. I was traumatized by what I had seen in the streets, and crushed beyond belief at the way the campaign and the convention were ending.

More violence occurred the following day. According to news reports, at 5 am the police and national guard raided the 15th floor, rounded up McCarthy staffers on various pretexts, clubbing people as they went, and herded them into the lobby, where the senator found them stunned and sitting on the floor when he arrived. He said a few words and sent them back to their rooms in small groups of three or four. Most of us were out of Chicago by the end of the day, wanting nothing more to do with Chicago, its mayor, or the Democratic Party. I headed back to St. Paul.

My house in Albany, Vermont, pop. 528

On the porch of my new home,
Fall 1970

Lake Willoughby, Westmore,
Vermont, October, 1972

Chapter Seven

Forging a New Life

1969-1977

I stayed only briefly in St. Paul. The situation there was pretty awful, and, at the urging of my parents, particularly my mother, who I think did not want me around to experience her deep depression and watch her slowly die, I continued on to New York City, leaving with her my Oklahoma-acquired cat Eric, whom she had grown fond of and had been caring for. I could have stayed longer in St. Paul and tried to help my parents out more, and I have regretted that I didn't do that despite their stated wishes. But they were very proud of the work I had been doing and both wanted me to get on with my life as a new college graduate.

I moved into Mark Siegel and Marty Munn's apartment on West 114th Street with another temporarily dislocated McCarthy campaigner, Barbara Lowe. There were too many of us in a small apartment, the relationships were complicated, and the arrangement ended not too terribly long after it began.

By October I had moved into an apartment on West 15th Street to room with yet another McCarthy campaign veteran, and had landed a job as a recreational therapist at Bronx State Hospital by virtue of having a B.A. in psychology. Bronx State was the teaching hospital of the New York state hospital system, was always innovating, and had just decided to establish a recreation department on the hospital's Montefiore unit, hiring six new college graduates to staff it.

As recreational therapists our job was to encourage our mentally ill patients to come out of the private mental worlds into which they had retreated, and to interact with each other and with us in the real one. Traditionally, the vehicle for this is almost any kind of interactive social or recreational activity, such as indoor board and card games, outdoor athletic activities, and dances and parties around one theme or another. Along with its new recreational therapists, however, Bronx State had decided to add dance therapy to the recreational therapies it would make available to its patients once the new staff was trained.

Unlike playing checkers or organizing a softball game, working with patients using dance therapy techniques required extensive training. We were fortunate to have as our trainers two very different but equally talented dancers and therapists, Miriam "Mimi" Berger, and Elissa Queyquep White. Both were passionate about their art and excellent teachers.

In lay person's language, the principle underlying dance therapy is that how individuals feel emotionally determines how they use the space around them, and conversely, that changing how individuals use the space around them can change how they feel. In the world of mental health work the severely ill patient who sits all day long nearly unmoving, arms crossed and fists clenched, is iconic, and we had no shortage of such individuals at Bronx State. Our challenge as fledgling dance therapists was to get those patients to open up physically so that they might open up mentally as well. The amazing thing was, it worked!

It interested me greatly to learn that an early adherent of dance therapy had been Rudolph Laban, a European architect, who found himself drawn to study the relationship between human beings and the space that surrounds them. I had been interested in architecture from childhood, sketching floor plans for houses when friends were jumping rope, and taking more pictures of buildings than of people with my first cameras. Therefore, this new connection between architecture and psychology, which I hadn't been aware of before, captured my interest as a possible vocational direction. I began to consider a future in environmental architecture, and began reading what some of the radical architects of the time had to say about the role of architecture in society. One of these was Buckminster Fuller; another was Paolo Soleri, who had just published *Arcology: The City in the Image of Man*.

In the midst of these changes and discoveries, my father called in early May 1969 to say it was time to come home and say goodbye to my mother. I brought with me a small white porcelain vase and a little bouquet of brightly colored paper flowers, as my mother was allergic to flowers and I didn't want to be so obvious about her imminent death as to bring her real ones.

I placed the vase on the bedside table in her hospital room, and it did manage to provide a bit of cheer. But during my last visit to the hospital before returning to New York, as I was leaving, a nurse knocked the vase off the table and it shattered on the floor. "Oh, don't worry," she said brightly, "you can bring another one next time." My mother and I looked at each other with tears in our eyes, and I could no longer keep from sobbing. We both knew there would be no next time, as we tightly hugged each other goodbye.

I never saw my mother again. Not long after my visit she was transferred to a nursing home, and died that night. My father believed that she had been hoarding a stash of pills, and had taken them to end her life.

*   *   *

I worked for another year at Bronx State before being accepted into the architecture program at Pratt Institute in Brooklyn, scheduled to enroll in the fall of 1970. But the longer I remained in New York, the less sure I was that I wanted to spend three more years there. It was a period of high crime in the city and I'd had it with always having to skulk around, wondering if I were about to be attacked or robbed. The apartment I had moved into on West 88th Street had been burglarized, and a week or so after it happened I'd turned back the corner of my mattress to change the sheets, only to discover a nylon stocking wrapped and knotted around a good sized rock, clearly having been meant for my head had I interrupted the crime. Three more years of this? I didn't think so.

The therapist I'd been seeing since my mother's death accused me of wanting to escape—to find a cute little house with a white picket fence around it, where I could live happily ever after. Perhaps she was right about the escape part. In any case, a cute little house with a white picket fence didn't seem like a bad idea at all compared to New York City right then.

I longed for the beauty and peacefulness I remembered from a trip to Vermont I'd taken a year earlier at the height of foliage season. I had saved up about $3,000—a considerable amount of money at that time—and figured I could live on that for quite a while outside of New York. I knew no one in Vermont and nothing about the state, but I thought if I started at the Massachusetts border and slowly headed north, I would find something I liked and could afford. Soon my thoughts had become a plan.

I can recall in detail only five stops I made on my journey north through Vermont. The first was in East Dummerston, near Putney, not too far into the state. The guest house on the 600-acre estate of Ellsworth Bunker was for rent, and I was intrigued. I knew Bunker was our ambassador to Vietnam, and that his Vermont estate had been the site of important diplomatic meetings over the years. The property was beautiful, but alas, well beyond my means. I continued on.

My second stop was at a nondescript building on Route 100, somewhere in the middle of the state, to see a second-floor apartment. Being ignorant of my surroundings, I didn't realize that I was in the middle of ski country, and that the rentals were all geared to weekend skiers or seasonal people who worked the mountains. What I do remember is that the apartment

I looked at didn't feel like a home, or even a potential home. I'm a pretty good nester, but there was something about the place that seemed devoid of any character I could build on.

I traveled on to Hardwick, and almost rented a large old Victorian house on a hill overlooking downtown. But something about the town stopped me. It seemed more dead than alive, and I couldn't imagine what I would ever find to do there.

After an equally fruitless stop in Greensboro, I made it back out to Route 14 and very soon reached the nearby town of Albany. The proprietor of the general store knew of a place for rent and directed me to the town's librarian, Ellen von Stackelberg, who conveniently was on duty at the library right next door. The house in question belonged to Ellen's daughter and her husband, who had moved to a larger town nearby, and wanted to rent it for $50 a month. That sounded pretty good to me.

The house was just off Route 14 on Water Street, next to a small orchard, and directly across from the Albany Volunteer Fire Department, housed in a slightly oversized and somewhat decrepit garage. The house looked great on the outside with a coat of fresh white paint and a nice front porch that wrapped around to one side. The inside was another story. The downstairs was brightly painted but stark in its emptiness and entirely lacking in amenities. It included a very large kitchen, a tiny parlor, a small living room, and a bathroom through which you had to pass to reach the stairs to the second floor. The upstairs rooms had all been gutted down to their single one-inch-thick board walls, as if someone had intended to renovate the entire second floor but didn't know what to do next.

It seemed a perfect place to start my new life. If I was looking for a blank slate, I had certainly found one. So I closed the deal verbally and returned to New York to pack up and make my move the following week. I was excited to be headed to Albany, Vermont, population 528, and for all practical purposes in the middle of nowhere.

Then disaster struck.

When I went to get in my car the day after I returned to New York, I couldn't find it. I circled the block, then circled the four adjacent blocks, before a horrible certainty came over me: I knew exactly where I had parked the car, and it wasn't there anymore.

The officer I spoke to when I called the New York Police Department was pleasant but not reassuring. "Volkswagen bug? That's a very popular car. It's probably in a hundred pieces by now, being sold for parts. I'll write up a report, but I wouldn't expect to see it again."

And I didn't.

Here I was, due to move to a very rural part of Vermont in a matter of days, and I had no way to get there, and no way to get around once I arrived. I knew very little about Albany, but I did know that no form of public transportation went anywhere near it. And even if I could somehow get there without a car, what would I do once I was there? The town consisted of two general stores, a very old grade school, Ellen's part-time library, and a funeral home. There was nothing to do but withdraw the savings on which I had planned to live and buy a car. So I plunked down most of the money I had in the world for a new VW bug.

I moved to Vermont on October 2, the same date I had started work at Bronx State two years earlier, and the same date I had taken my first trip to Vermont with my coworker Alice, to celebrate our one-year anniversary of having worked at the hospital. Alice and our mutual friend Phyllis, another recreational therapist at Bronx State, drove up behind me in Phyllis' car to help with the move and check out the scene.

We had a grand weekend and Alice, ever the romantic, left me with a few things she felt essential to my resettlement in Vermont: a cast-iron frying pan, a little metal basket with garlic in it, a muff that had belonged to her great-grandmother, and a small rocking chair. We drank a lot of wine and did a lot of house cleaning.

The day after they left, I began to explore. My nose led me almost immediately to Philip Hoff's Orleans County U.S. Senate campaign office in the Hotel Newport, where I left a note for its absent staff person, David LaRoche, summarizing my political experience and offering to help. Hoff was familiar to me as a political figure who had broken with the Democratic establishment to oppose the Vietnam war in 1968 when he was governor of Vermont, and had endorsed Gene McCarthy after Bobby Kennedy's death.

LaRoche stopped by my house the next day and after a short conversation quickly signed me on to the Hoff field staff at $15/week for the last month of the campaign.

There are few better ways to learn a new town or area than by door-to-door canvassing. I've done it twice now in new places I'd just moved to, and both times it paved my way into the life of the community. The Hoff campaign was the first such time, and was an excellent introduction to the "Northeast Kingdom," or "NEK," the three northeastern counties in the state where I was to live for most of the next fifty-odd years.

In 1970, as is still mostly true today, Orleans, Essex, and Caledonia counties were remarkably poor, white, and rural. They had the usual smattering of small retail businesses that support small towns of any size—gas stations, general stores, and sometimes what used to be called "dime stores"—but no one was making a great deal of money since the local consuming public had little to spend.

As I explored Newport, the town of any size closest to me, located just five miles from the Canadian border, I often heard French being spoken on the streets, and learned from David that it was the language of choice for the older generation of French Canadian immigrants and many of their adult children, who had populated these northern counties.

Conventional wisdom would have it that because I had so little in common with the poor, rural, largely French Canadian population of Newport, I would have had a difficult time gaining acceptance and being effective among them. But once again that turned out not to be the case. Although Hoff ultimately lost Orleans County, I received a warm welcome.

The people I met through the Hoff campaign were honest, hard working, and plainspoken, and rewarded those same simple virtues when they found them in others. For some reason Irene Beaudry trusted me almost immediately, and took me under her wing. I'm sure that many of those who considered themselves the Northeast Kingdom's elite would have found it odd that I considered this an asset, but it was.

Irene, her husband Romeo, and their seven children lived not far from my house in Albany, just outside the village on a back hill in a house devoid of almost any item that might make a person's life easier. Romeo was disabled, and their source of income at the time when they were caring for young children was public assistance. In a village made up largely of small farmers and lower-wage working people struggling to look as if they were financially better off than they were, if on occasion I would mention to my new neighbors that I'd been up visiting the Beaudrys, I could sense they found that rather strange.

Irene, however, was very bright, very knowledgeable, and willing to share what she knew. She would later go on to get her GED and then a B.A., and go to work for the Vermont Department of Vocational Rehabilitation as an effective advocate for her clients. At the time I knew her best, her mission in life was advocating on behalf of those living in poverty in the Northeast Kingdom as president of the NEK's Low Income Association (LIA). This was a group of low-income residents organized under the auspices of the Orleans County Council of Social Agencies (OCCSA), a federally funded community action agency established as part of President Lyndon Johnson's War on Poverty. Based in Newport with a satellite office in St. Johnsbury, OCCSA served the entire tri-county area.

I began attending LIA meetings as a Hoff campaign organizer, and continued going to meetings after the election just because they interested me. After a while I became a dues-paying member, but I was still taken by surprise when Irene asked me one day if I would be willing to represent the NEK chapter on the statewide Vermont Low Income Advocacy Council (VLIAC). By then I was employed by the Vermont Department of Social Welfare (DSW), so many of the LIA families I knew were also my clients. I had gotten to know their hardships and challenges quite intimately, and had become a champion for them within the office bureaucracy. Apparently they appreciated my commitment to their welfare and recognized my passion for social justice on a broader scale, thought they could make good use of my education and political skills, and wouldn't take no for an answer. Thus began my long association with VLIAC and with OCCSA, whose deputy director, Jim Keeney, I would meet and marry years later.

My arrival in northern Vermont in 1970 came at the same time as a large "back-to-the-land" movement of mostly well-educated young people, ably described in Kate Daloz's book, *We Are As Gods.*[13] Most of them had yet to appear in the workforce, having either a private source of financial support or preferring to live off the land with the help of food stamps. In a small number of cases single parents relied on what is commonly known as "welfare," Aid to Needy Families with Children, or ANFC. Most of my colleagues at the office didn't know quite what to make of me, and wondered if I were one of those "hippies" they'd heard about; but they seemed glad to have me there to lighten their workload regardless. For my part, I was glad to have a meaningful job that paid me more than enough to meet my needs.

I enjoyed my work at DSW and felt I got along with everyone very well, coworkers and clients alike, and was able to bridge many of the differences between them. The staff trusted me, and because of this, I was allowed to try new things.

---

[13] Kate Daloz, *We Are As Gods: Back to the Land in the 1970s on the Quest for a New America* (PublicAffairs, 2016).

One of the first issues I sought to address was the inability of many of the large families we worked with to keep their children adequately clothed with the amount of money they were allotted on public assistance. Over the initial objections of some of the older staff, district manager Mabel Ayer gave me permission to start a free clothing depot in the basement of the building. It quickly became a big hit.

Word of this resource spread fast and both donations and needy moms and dads flowed in and out all day long, soon necessitating the depot's move to a larger space. Unfortunately, our clients seemed not to be considered the deserving poor, and most of the empty spaces we thought would be good locations turned out to be strangely unavailable.

Eventually the depot moved to the dark, damp, and unfinished cavernous basement of St. Mary Star of the Sea Catholic Church, where a dirt floor, stone foundation walls, and a low ceiling made it feel something like a medieval prison. Nonetheless, those in need of clothes for their children continued to patronize it, and once I negotiated with OCCSA to staff it on a part-time basis with community VISTAs (Volunteers in Service to America), it somehow managed to become a welcoming space.

Next, I took on the matter of eyeglasses. At the time eyeglasses were not an authorized medical expense under the state's Medicaid program, and the only way a low-income person could get glasses was through the local Lions Club, which was very generous, but often unable to meet the demand.

Along with the failure to fund dental care and dentures, the state's policy with respect to eyeglasses seemed very short sighted to me, for while conservative legislators and taxpayers alike regularly called for mythical "welfare cheats" to get off welfare and get a job, they seemed unable to understand that people who couldn't see properly were unable to perform most kinds of work, and that people with rotten teeth or no teeth at all would never be hired for any position in which they had to interact with the public.

Then there were the children, for whom good vision was essential to success in school, to staying in school, and to securing any chance they might have to break out of the cycle of poverty that held their families in its grasp. It all seemed pretty obvious to me, so I laid out the problem in a letter and started a fundraising campaign to create a pool of money to fund the purchase of eyeglasses for our clients.

We were having a good bit of success from a sympathetic public when Mabel called me into her office one day and said the fundraising had to stop. Lloyd Selby, president of the Derby Line Bank, had received one of my letters, and though he had been happy to approve the bank's contribution, which we had already received, he had also phoned Governor Deane Davis to find out why the Department of Social Welfare's Newport office was running a private fundraising campaign, and why—more to the point—the department's budget didn't include money to purchase eyeglasses for people who needed them. Apparently it didn't sit well with the governor to have his budget questioned in this way, so his response was to call Mabel and say that the fundraising had to stop.

My territory as an ANFC caseworker was enormous, encompassing the entire 721 square miles of Orleans County, plus the sparsely populated northern half of the 675-square-mile Essex County, which didn't have enough residents to support an office of its own. Regulations at the time required home visits by their caseworker to every family on ANFC twice a year. I valued the visits, as they gave me an opportunity to get to know my clients much better than I would have from the opposite side of a desk surrounded by partitions that afforded no privacy at all. During our conversations I came to understand the social and economic challenges that each particular family faced in a way I never would have otherwise.

In many instances it was only during a long, intimate, personal visit over a cup of coffee that I would get information about a child's special educational needs that were being ignored at school, or about something a working mother needed for her job and couldn't afford. Often these were things I could do something about under the department's existing policies, and if not, I was free to advocate on my clients' behalf with the department or other agencies. It sold me on the value of home visits, and on the importance of taking a holistic approach to the needs of client families. Unfortunately, both the visits and the ability to take a holistic approach to an entire family have long since been abandoned by the current social welfare system, to the detriment of its clients.

When I began my work at DSW, most of what I knew and thought about poverty came from books, or from the few low-income people I had worked with in other contexts. Now it was the focus of my work and I was seeing it up close. A few families on my caseload still lived in homes that included a room with a dirt floor. On a first visit to one client's home, I remember having difficulty locating the house, because the directions led me to a structure that I couldn't believe was actually sheltering a family through a Vermont winter.

Many of my clients' refrigerators and cupboards were painfully bare, as they voluntarily showed me, or as I could see with my own eyes when they were opened to reach the milk and sugar for the cup of coffee that was always offered. It amazed me that these mothers—and most of my adult clients *were* mothers—could provide for their children on the amount of money the state was giving them. I understood why there were often chickens, pigs, or goats outside in pens or wandering around freely, being raised to supplement the store-bought food supply.

Other families I visited lived in much better conditions, and some of these mothers worked, at least part time. Often their poverty had resulted from the death of a spouse or divorce, and their life had been middle class or at least working class until it plummeted into poverty with the wage-earner's disappearance. While these women generally had more "things" in their home, and often very nice things left over from their former lives, they had no more money than my multi-generationally poor clients, and often many fewer survival skills. But they were trying to cope and keep their heads up when they had to do things that visibly labeled them as "poor," like proffering food stamps in their local grocery stores. I considered both groups of mothers real heroes.

I had just as much interest in those on my caseload whom I thought of as the voluntary poor—the so-called hippies who had moved to Vermont determined to live off the land but were not quite able to make it without some financial help from the state. Many of my new neighbors assumed that I was also a hippie—whatever they thought a hippie was—so I was very curious to know more about what it actually meant to be one.

These young unmarried women who had given birth to children were as legally entitled to assistance as anyone else on ANFC, but were much more like me in background. They were my age, many were college graduates, and nearly all of them had also come to Vermont from somewhere else. Like them, I had been on food stamps myself for three and a half months when I first moved to Vermont and unexpectedly had no money; and as I'm sure was the case with many of them, my father would certainly have helped me out if I'd asked him, but I wanted to be independent.

My status as a food stamp recipient hadn't seemed to bother anyone in the DSW office when I'd applied for my job there; when I was hired they joked that they'd do anything to get a client "off the dole." I told myself that I'd been looking hard for work at the time and had only become poor through the catastrophe of my car theft, and that was true. But really, I wondered, was I any different from my hippie clients other than not having a child to support? Wasn't it just about the choices we had voluntarily made and where those circumstances had led us? I suspected so.

Because of my age and my obvious willingness to deal with the transplanted Vermonters, my supervisor made an exception to the usual alphabetical assignment of clients and decided to assign me anyone on our ANFC caseload at Earth People's Park in Norton, almost an hour's drive from our office. In a 1970 article in *Playboy*, Richard Pollak estimated that there were over 35,000 hippies in Vermont at the time I worked for DSW, and that they accounted for roughly a third of the 107,527 people in the state between the ages of 18 and 34.[14] Many lived collectively in various group living arrangements, but none of the households, communes, or communities was as large or as controversial as Earth People's Park, a 55-acre tract of land on the Canadian border at Norton.

When I was sent to the Park as a caseworker in 1971 conditions were very primitive. Shelters of all sorts were lined up in crooked rows along muddy trails, tents next to lean-tos next to teepees next to shacks next to vehicles both capable of transit and not. There was no water, power, or septic service at the site, and in this pre-cell-phone era no telephone service either. And, no trash removal. In the warmer months, when the resident population swelled, the place had an odor all its own.

One ANFC client at the Park who left a lasting impression on me was a pregnant teenage girl living in a teepee with an older man. Finding them was a bit of a feat, since there were no real roads through the Park and certainly no street addresses on the shelters, but I managed to locate her. The man was suspicious of me, just this side of hostile, but I sensed that the girl was nervous about her pregnancy and wanted to talk, so I told her I had some extra time and asked if she might like a ride out to pick up groceries or other things she might need. We ended up spending a couple of hours together before returning.

I drove her over to the hospital in Lancaster, New Hampshire, and showed her where she could go to give birth. I encouraged her to get the prenatal care to which she was entitled under Medicaid, and showed her where she could go for that. Her face relaxed with relief that "the state worker" was not only saying that she *could* do these things, but that it was perfectly alright. Even though I was not much older than she was and had never been pregnant myself,

---

[14] Richard Pollak, "Taking Over Vermont," *Playboy* 19:4 (1972).

I definitely felt like her mother, and felt badly returning her to her teepee at the end of our afternoon together. I could only hope she would take my advice.

It seemed to me that I was more than fairly paid for my work, and as I had minimal expenses, I soon felt I had things well in hand again financially. After six months in Albany I had asked my father for a loan, and for $5,800 bought a small, one-and-a-half-story house just outside of Derby Village on five acres of land along the Clyde River. The house wasn't much to speak of but the location was perfect: It was walking distance to the center of town on a short, quiet dirt road that ran behind the drive-in movie on a hill above it, and just a five-mile drive into Newport. My monthly mortgage payment was $60. I still had a more than sufficient professional wardrobe from my days in New York, and not much else to spend my salary on other than food and the weekly Friday night out at Gantry's.

So, when it came time for my annual evaluation and my performance entitled me to a significant raise, I couldn't see the point and declined it, stating that the people I worked with needed the money far more than I did, and asking instead that it be credited back to the department's budget. This caused quite a furor when it got back to the higher-ups, and the matter was referred to the state treasurer for resolution. He deemed my request impossible to grant and suggested I just donate some money to my favorite charity, which I did. It was a memorable lesson in the inability of a bureaucracy to temper its rules and regulations with common sense.

*　　　　*　　　　*

During this period of the early 1970s I had begun to develop a sense that my brain was atrophying. I had gone from the intense environment of Bronx State, with its daily schedule of meetings and conferences and demanding experiential training in group process and group psychodynamics, to a far less verbal or analytic environment, and I felt it mentally.

Not that I wasn't finding my job at DSW rewarding—I was. And in my free time I was developing an interesting circle of friends, with whose help I was learning how to live a productive rural life that was partially sustained by growing vegetables and raising animals. But when someone passed my name on to the National Women's Political Caucus (NWPC) in early 1972, and they called to ask if I'd be interested in doing some fieldwork for them until the 1972 national political conventions, I couldn't resist. I quit my job and headed for Washington, D.C.

Although most women's rights advocates are feminists who become politicized, my path to the women's movement went in the other direction, from my political organizing work to my awareness of myself as a woman with a stake in feminist issues.

When I left the Northeast Kingdom in 1972 to join the staff of the NWPC, I frankly didn't have much practical or theoretical knowledge about what's called the Second Wave of feminism. I had left New York City just as the women's movement was beginning to pick up steam in cities and on college campuses, and the people I was surrounded by in the Northeast Kingdom were either not yet aware that there was a women's movement, or had rejected it as not relevant to their lives.

Once I arrived in Washington, my own ignorance of the movement quickly became a thing of the past. The Caucus had just been founded in 1971 by some of the most high-powered political women in the country. I was suddenly surrounded by bright and committed feminists of every size and shape, from the NWPC's leadership, whose names read like a who's who in feminist thought and action,[15] to newly militant housewives in places like Tucson, Arizona; Salem, Oregon; and Austin, Texas.

---

[15]The NWPC's founders included former Congresswoman and president of Women USA Bella Abzug; Liz Carpenter, former press secretary to First Lady Lady Bird Johnson; Shirley Chisholm, the first Black woman elected to Congress; Fannie Lou Hamer, community organizer and leader in the Civil Rights Movement; LaDonna Harris, Native American rights leader; Dorothy Height, president of the National Council of Negro

One of the first goals of the new organization was to increase the presence of women at all levels of government, and toward that end an educational arm of the organization called WEDS—Women's Education for Delegate Selection—had been created to be eligible for broader funding. It was WEDS that technically employed me.

The immediate goal of WEDS was to increase the number of women in state delegations to the 1972 Democratic and Republican conventions, so that those delegations would better reflect the population of their states than they had in 1968. In the case of the Democrats, the process to be followed had been laid out in detail in the 1969 *McGovern-Fraser Commission Guidelines*, adopted after the disastrous '68 convention. The *Guidelines* reformed the party's nominating process, which had allowed Hubert Humphrey to claim the nomination for president without ever having run in a single primary. Delegate selection procedures on the Republican side remained a bit looser and vaguer, but many Republican women across the country were calling for equal representation with just as loud a voice.

The NWPC had put together a small staff for WEDS guided by Doris Meissner, who would go on to become head of the U.S. Immigration and Naturalization Service under President Bill Clinton. My job was to prepare materials on each state's delegate selection procedures and distribute them to the local women who were organizing around this effort across the country. We also needed to develop a communications network to monitor each state party's delegate selection efforts as they unfolded, so we could identify where our help was most needed.

Where women were already organized and active, I was to work with selected states—Missouri, Texas, Illinois, and New Hampshire—to help put

---

Women; Ann Lewis, political director of the Democratic National Committee; Congresswoman Eleanor Holmes Norton, former chair of the Equal Employment Opportunity Commission; Elly Peterson, former vice chair of the Republican National Committee; U.S. Civil Rights Commissioner Jill Ruckelshaus; and Gloria Steinem, founding editor of *Ms.* magazine.

together what were often the first statewide NWPC meetings and then lead workshops in delegate selection procedures when those meetings were convened. In other states, including my home states of Minnesota and Vermont, I merely represented the national office at NWPC meetings and conventions. Finally, I was to prepare testimony on women's needs, including the need for an Equal Rights Amendment, for the Platform Committees of both parties.

I traveled a great deal, staying with a high school friend when I was in D.C., but otherwise living out of a suitcase in the homes of sympathetic women who were local NWPC members.

My most intense work was in Arizona, where early steps to select delegates had already assured the exclusion of most women, and where my job was to assist with research, documentation, and preparation of what would be the first legal challenge to the legitimacy of a state delegation based on the *McGovern-Fraser Commission Guidelines.* I spent a great deal of time working on their challenge with a local woman attorney and the Tucson NWPC chapter women. I'd never spent much time in the southwest before, and it was then and there that my lifetime affinity for the desert began.

I also spent quite a bit of time in Texas, memorable for a lunch with Liz Carpenter at her home to get her thoughts about how and where my organizing time could best be spent, then helping to organize Texas' rousing first state women's convention, and especially for the time I was able to spend with Frances "Sissy" Farenthold, then a Texas state legislator, who in a few months would be a serious candidate for nomination as vice president of the United States on the Democratic ticket.

My last assignment was to testify before the Platform Committee of the Democratic Party on the Equal Rights Amendment and women's needs. I packed my bags and flew to Boston to appear before the committee when it convened in Faneuil Hall. My work with WEDS then over, I headed home to Vermont.

*　　　　　*　　　　　*

W hat to do next? Considering the fact that I had five jobs over the next five years, I think it's safe to say that I had no clear idea about what I wanted to do with my life when I returned from Washington.

I first went to work for Community College of Vermont, in its infancy at the time, as its only Newport-area staff person. For about a year I recruited teachers, found classroom space, enrolled students, and helped those students translate their life experience into potential college credits. It lacked a challenge. When by June 1973 the state had completed its creation of the sprawling new Agency of Human Services (AHS) and was looking to fill the position of Newport resource coordinator in its new Division of Social and Rehabilitation Services, I applied and was hired.

This was right up my alley. I loved the challenge of being in a newly created position in a newly created division of a newly created agency, and being tasked with the design and implementation of an office that would support the agency's direct-service providers. I was beginning to realize that in terms of transferable employment skills, this was where my talents lay: in getting new programs off the ground and operational. Not unlike political campaigns, the work requires a clear vision of what things should look like in the end, a good idea of how best to get there, then a high intensity of effort and good collaboration with all stakeholders.

But the more experience I had with the new agency structure, which in keeping with a national trend had separated the determination of eligibility for financial assistance from the delivery of social services, the less I thought it served our clients well. Eligibility workers were assumed to need less education and training than caseworkers, and were selected accordingly and paid less. The result was that critically important first interviews with new clients became a matter of shuffling numbers, and no longer included a good initial diagnosis of the issues underlying the family's financial situation so that helpful referrals could be made. This in turn caused clients to miss out on important opportunities, and allowed problems to become emergencies.

As engagement in family casework lost its importance, and people with problems no longer had an opportunity to get help or advice from the same person or even the same office that helped them initially, nonprofit organizations sprang up offering specialized services on a privatized basis. This further fractured the provision of services to the same family and sometimes to the same individual, making it difficult for workers from either the public or private sectors to develop viable and effective service plans.

As the agency's resource coordinator, I set about to see what I could do to improve things, and established what I called the Newport Resource Group, which became the prototype for similar groups around the state. All it was, really, was a monthly meeting where staff from various divisions and departments of AHS could come together to talk to each other and to relevant staff from the private nonprofit organizations operating in their part of the state. Meetings typically began with sharing information on program changes, new benefits, and new staff. Next would be an in-depth presentation on a new program or resource to be sure that everyone understood what it had to offer, who was eligible, and how it could be accessed. Social workers could pick up a lot of information at these meetings and do some serious networking on behalf of their clients.

Of course, some just came for the coffee and doughnuts; but even that had an effect on the ease with which future referrals were made and accepted. It was a simple meeting, and it worked well at enhancing communication and fostering better service delivery. Many of these groups continued to meet and follow essentially the same format for decades. Once the resource unit and the resource group were up and running smoothly, I left the job, turning it over to my very able assistant, who ran it for many years afterwards.

I was happy to have the summer off and spent quite a bit of it riding around the back roads of the Northeast Kingdom with my boyfriend. He was part of a group of craftspeople, artists, and professional dancers from around Hartford, Connecticut, and New York City who had purchased a farm and considerable acreage in East Charleston, Vermont. By the time I got to know them they had evolved from a commune into a stable community. The boyfriend and I didn't last long as a couple, but my friendship with the members of the community did, and eventually I became a nonresident member myself and owner of a cabin there. Today Mad Brook Farm boasts seventeen houses, a state-of-the-art dance studio, and a third generation of residents.

But when Planned Parenthood of Vermont decided to open a clinic in Newport in September 1974, I was ready to go back to work again and became the Newport center coordinator, working under an old friend who had been both a former DSW client and a Low Income Association colleague, and who was now Planned Parenthood's area director for the Northeast Kingdom. Once again, I was setting up a new office, training and supervising a clinic staff of ten part-time family planning workers, and scheduling and overseeing the clinics.

Our two doctors, other than being men, were perfect for the job: young, friendly, and willing to roll with the punches to make things work. I remember one client we had who tested as anemic, but who refused the doctor's suggestion that she take iron pills, out of a general mistrust of anything that came from a pharmacy. The doctor's clever solution was to have her go to the hardware store and buy some nails, let them soak in water until they rusted, and then drink the water. She returned after a month of doing this with her iron at a normal level—problem solved! We ran four to six clinics each month for about nine months, until funding issues forced Planned Parenthood to close the office.

During this period, I was enjoying the life of a single woman in her late twenties in the Northeast Kingdom. There was a close-knit group of us who often hung out at Walt's Corner, a popular and successful book and music store in Newport owned and operated by two of the group. We drank and danced at

Gantry's on Friday nights after work, and had potluck suppers and dance parties on the weekends. We found and lost romantic partners periodically, but every now and then a relationship stuck, marriages were celebrated, new homes constructed, and babies were born and delighted over. Some of us lived alone in houses or apartments, others in communes or other forms of co-housing that did not share finances. Increasingly, many of us had jobs or businesses in the "straight" world, while others remained in the counterculture. It was an eclectic group, to say the least.

Living respectfully on the land was a new, shared experience of ours and an important one that was closely tied to the rural life we now led. It was not surprising, therefore, that the political work I did in Vermont during this time was as one of the organizers of a group called the Citizen's Caucus of Orleans County, which set about to educate local people on the new and very controversial land-use planning law that had just been passed, Act 250. The goal of the legislation was to promote economic development, but to assure that it happened in a way that protected Vermont's natural resources and special character.

Working with local legislators, we organized and promoted a series of public meetings at which the legislators would present a panel discussion on the new law and then field questions from the audience. We felt strongly that planning was the way to protect what we all loved most about Vermont, but it was a ticklish situation. The obvious and very understandable retort from many conservative lifelong Vermont farmers and loggers was: Who the hell are you to tell us what to protect and how to do it? As newcomers to the state we were not in a particularly strong position in this debate, but the goal of the legislation made sense to enough people, and Act 250 has survived, though after all these years it remains controversial.

I was ready to go back to work again in the fall of 1975 and needed the money. When I'd left Planned Parenthood, I had thought there must be a way for me to live without working, which it seemed to me so many of my new friends were doing. But by fall I had figured out that you can live without working but not without money, and that many of those seemingly self-sufficient friends were either independently wealthy, on some degree of public assistance, or growing and selling marijuana. I had just about exhausted all the obvious places to work in Newport, so when I saw an ad for an administrator of the YWCA Child Care Center in St. Johnsbury, forty-two miles to the south, I applied.

I was hired to be the center's administrator by Bonnie Griffin, a woman I'd seen make an exciting presentation on holistic medical care for children at a conference in Island Pond years before. Bonnie was a St. Johnsbury native, a mover and shaker in the social service and health worlds there, and a nurse practitioner who had helped found and organize a trio of important resources for her area: the Child Health Center in Dr. David Toll's pediatric office; Umbrella, a private nonprofit that supported victims of domestic violence and sexual assault; and the YWCA Child Care Center.

It was through this job that I met my husband, Jim Keeney. When I first heard of Jim, he was somewhat notorious in the St. Johnsbury area as a divorced ladies' man who lived fast and loose and was a co-owner of The Drawing Room, a popular bar under the Portland Street bridge that served excellent hamburgers cooked by his daughter Dorigen. The bar catered to anyone and everyone without exception, until someone—believed to be a disgruntled mentally ill patron—burned the place down in the summer of 1973.

When I met Jim two years after the fire, however, the reputation didn't quite seem to fit. He was then the deputy director of OCCSA, managing the community action agency's operations in Caledonia and southern Essex Counties from its St. Johnsbury office, and directing its Comprehensive Employment & Training Act (CETA) program throughout the Northeast Kingdom, responsible for over 100 enrollees and around $30 million dollars of annual budget. That size program was big stuff in the Northeast Kingdom, and it led to our first meeting.

The Child Care Center needed another staff person and sought to have the position paid for through CETA. I walked down to Jim's office one day to negotiate, and left intrigued. He was neither the bureaucrat nor the passionate nonprofit administrator-with-a-mission that I'd expected; instead I found a rumpled, laid-back guy in his early 40s, who seemed surprisingly casual about my request and assured me that he could come up with the slot I needed. He said yes, it was fine to go ahead and advertise the position, without any more ado.

Once having met, Jim and I began seeing each other and married in 1978. He had gotten his B.A. and M.A. in history from the University of Wisconsin nearly a generation ahead of my enrollment there, and been an A.B.D. in Columbia University's Ph.D. program. We complement each other quite well politically, having exactly the same politics and values, he on an intellectual and theoretical level, I on an activist one. And there is almost no person I can think of about whom we do not have the same opinion, which I have always found rather amazing.

I got my additional CETA slot but was not at the Child Care Center much longer, and moved into a CETA slot myself as a vocational counselor at Northeast Kingdom Mental Health Service back in Newport. My task was to develop jobs in the community for the developmentally disabled and sometimes mentally ill clients I worked with, and to support them in whatever way necessary once they left our sheltered workshop and entered the real world of work.

Most of my clients were young men in their late 20s and early 30s who had led very limited lives, often surrounded by well-meaning but overprotective families, sometimes families who had tried to keep them as hidden as possible from public view.

As I worked with these young men it seemed to me that if they could successfully transition to regular jobs in the community, they might also have the ability to live more independent lives in general, with whatever degree of support they needed. So, in consultation with their counselors, family members, and others at the agency, I set out to find an understanding landlord or two who would be willing to rent to our clients. I had success with this, and two of our clients became the first two such men the agency had ever helped move into independent housing, a goal that is now taken almost for granted.

I thought Mental Health to be a well-run agency and hoped to stay there awhile, but it was not to be; a year and a half later, when the CETA slot ran out, I found myself unemployed once again. By that time I had been working in direct service or low-level administrative positions at social service agencies in the Northeast Kingdom for seven years. If there were agencies I hadn't worked *for,* I had certainly worked *with* them through mutual clients or interagency collaboratives.

I had gotten to know many people with many needs, for whom I was or had been a caseworker, group worker, counselor, advocate, neighbor, advisor, friend, colleague, or client at one time or another, and often more than one of those things at the same time. It was an experience unique to the time and place. What I learned about public agencies and nonprofit organizations from that experience is that they are all pretty much the same. Each has its strengths and weaknesses, and particular things that it can or cannot do for its clients. But basically, it is only the individuals who work in these offices, and the degree to which they create a culture of advocacy, that is different. Good advocacy is almost always what's required to solve any problem, and good advocates are as good as gold.

Newlyweds, June 23, 1978, Newbury, Vermont

Chapter Eight

Finding My Voice

1979-1981

All those years of helping people solve, over and over again, different aspects of what was essentially the same problem—their inability to escape a hierarchical economic system that kept them at the bottom—made me think that there must be a more efficient way to attack the essential challenge they shared. I decided to go to law school. When I applied to law school my fantasy was that I would graduate, buy a small Airstream trailer that I could outfit as a mobile law office, then ride circuit around the Northeast Kingdom helping entire classes of people achieve legal and social justice with each case I brought to court.

I was accepted at Vermont Law School and two months after marrying Jim in June 1978 I was back in school after a ten-year hiatus. I was a bit of an oddity. At the age of thirty-three I was considered a nontraditional student, and I was also a commuting Vermonter, also very much a minority position at VLS. Rather than ignoring me, however, my fellow students seemed to appreciate the fact that I already had a useful body of life experience that most of them still lacked, and I was elected to the board of trustees representing the Class of 1981.

I took my responsibility as a trustee seriously, probably far more seriously than was intended, and in addition to attending meetings I vowed to be a bridge between the student body and the board. Toward that end I interviewed as many of the trustees as I could, and wrote a column, "Trustee Profiles" for the VLS newspaper. My goal was to humanize the highly influential individuals who were setting the course of our brand-new law school and helping to establish its reputation, on which we would all depend when we graduated and went looking for work.

By late 1979 I felt I had established enough of a relationship with my fellow trustees to proffer an opinion on an important matter, so when the agenda arrived for our October meeting, indicating that we would be considering new nominees for trustee, I sat down and wrote a letter to Hon. Sterry Waterman, then president of the board as well as senior judge of the Second Circuit Court of Appeals, recommending Frances "Sissy" Farenthold for the position.

Since I'd met her in Texas, Farenthold had become the president of Wells College. An attorney, wife, and mother, and a social and political leader of national prominence, she had received her undergraduate degree from Vassar and her JD from the University of Texas Law School. She had served as a member of the Texas House of Representatives while a practicing attorney, and in the early 1970s had made a credible if unsuccessful bid to become governor of Texas. In 1972 her name had been placed in nomination to be the Democratic Party's candidate for vice president of the United States, and she had received the second highest number of votes. Farenthold had also served as chair of the National Women's Political Caucus prior to her selection for the presidency of Wells. I believed she could make a unique and valuable contribution to Vermont Law School, and in my letter to Waterman touted her as an excellent role model for women law students in particular.

I had assumed that Waterman would pass my recommendation on to the rest of the trustees, but in retrospect I can see that I got several things wrong in proposing Farenthold's selection as I did. First of all, if we were going to be voting on this matter at our late October meeting, I'm sure that a candidate had already been handpicked by October 12, when I received the agenda and decided to recommend her. Second, Waterman was probably the wrong person with whom to entrust my recommendation. For one thing he was a Republican, and Farenthold a liberal Democrat. Better choices for the recipient of my letter might have been Betty Fishman, the only female member of the board at that time other than we two student trustees, or Norm Redlich, also a Democrat and dean of the New York University School of Law.

In any case nothing came of my suggestion; but the effort was not a total loss, as my relationship with Judge Waterman became closer. When I graduated two years later and it was time to start studying for the Vermont bar exam, he very generously gave me a key to his office in the St. Johnsbury federal building so that I could come and go at my convenience. I had given birth to Elizabeth over Christmas vacation my last year in law school, and he no doubt guessed correctly that finding time to study at home might be difficult while juggling the needs of a six-month-old baby.

Although I entered law school with the idea of becoming a circuit-riding attorney, by the time I graduated in May 1981 what I wanted was to become a judge. My goal was the same in both cases: doing justice. But where my interest in the law prior to law school had been to right wrongs through legal advocacy at a faster pace than social work allowed, my three years at VLS had taught me that an even surer way to accomplish my desired end would be through appointment as a judge.

I had grown fascinated with the tension between the law as a codification of societal norms on the one hand, and as a force by which people's behavior could be shaped, on the other. While people need to know clearly what society expects of them and what the consequences will be if they fail to conform to the law, it became clear to me the more I studied it that the law was a constantly evolving and dynamic force, not a static one. I concluded that it was in the writing of legal decisions, and at the appellate level especially, that this evolution occurred, and where the inherent tension between predictability and doing justice gets resolved.

I was particularly interested in how this tension would play out in the areas of labor law and family law, in which I had concentrated my studies. Labor law had interested me since my undergraduate study of intellectual history and labor history at the University of Minnesota. This interest was revived and given a professional foundation at VLS through the tutelage of Professor Jack McCrory, who recognized my strong interest in the field and during the spring semester of my third year arranged an internship for me in the attorney general's office, assisting in the preparation of cases going before the Vermont Labor Relations Board. My interest in family law, of course, stemmed from my previous career as a social worker, and my continuing commitment to help struggling families.

Complicating my career plan was the reality of my present life. In late 1977, at the age of 64, my father had been diagnosed with Alzheimer's Disease. At the time he was living in Roseville, Minnesota, with a woman he had known for some time and who was now living with him in his condominium. Neither my brother nor I trusted her intentions, which seemed to be to live off his generosity without making any commitment or contribution of her own.

When my father's condition worsened he began attending an adult day program near his home, but even that wasn't working out from his companion's perspective, and during Christmas vacation of my first year in law school I received a hysterical call from her demanding that I come get my father because she couldn't stand living with him anymore. With his safety my first consideration, I flew out to the Twin Cities, packed up what I thought he'd need for a short stay, and bought us an overnight train ticket back to Vermont in a sleeper car compartment.

I had carefully locked the compartment door but awoke in the night to find my father missing. With the help of a porter ("Little man in pajamas? Oh yes, he went that way"), I eventually found him several cars forward, walking with no purpose, and with no slippers on his feet. I got him turned around and we started back to our car, braving the January cold each time we went from one car to another. "God damn it," my father muttered as his bare feet crossed the cold metal expansion plates, "why don't they turn on the heat in here?"

My father spent the next twelve years until his death in Vermont, moving in with us initially, but having to accept nursing home care eventually. Though we tried repeatedly to cobble together other solutions, resources for Alzheimer's patients were few and far between and nothing seemed adequate to keep him safe. Meanwhile, the woman he had been living with confirmed our suspicions by bringing a palimony suit against him for ownership of his condominium. The lawsuit was eventually thrown out, but not before we spent what money he had left defending him.

Despite the personal agony of watching my father deteriorate and the necessary trips to Minnesota for depositions and ultimately for the hearing, I did well at VLS and was awarded the American Jurisprudence Awards in both Labor Law and Family Law when I graduated. During my last semester I was encouraged to apply for a judicial clerkship, the opportunity to work for a Vermont judge for one year after graduation, and in December I was invited to interview with the Hon. Albert W. Barney, chief justice of the Vermont Supreme Court.

I had never met the chief justice and had no idea what my chances were. VLS was a new and untested law school, and no VLS graduate had yet been accepted for a clerkship with Vermont's highest court. There was also my gender to worry about. The Court had only selected male clerks in recent years and I would be interviewing for the clerkship in my ninth month of pregnancy. No way would I be able to downplay my gender.

I arrived for my interview looking a bit like a giant beach ball with arms and legs. Someone of short stature does not generally carry a pregnancy well, and I had gained 65 pounds. There was only one place for all that weight to go, and that was out in front of me.

Anthony Otis, then deputy clerk of the Court, ushered me into his office for a pre-interview and offered me a chair. I knew the moment I sat down and sank into the comfort of the soft, plush cushion that there was no way I was ever going to be able to get up and out of it without looking like a complete fool. Otis grasped the situation and handled it as professionally as possible, coming out from behind his desk at the conclusion of our meeting to say with a tiny smile that he knew he couldn't comment on my physical condition, so he was just going to excuse himself to see if the chief justice was ready for me. With that he left his office and shut the door firmly, allowing me to extricate myself as best I could.

The interview with Chief Justice Barney went well and I was offered the job, which would begin the following August. All I had to do was have the baby, graduate from law school, and take and pass the bar exam. I would later learn that I was only the third female Supreme Court law clerk in Vermont history, and the first to clerk for a chief justice.

Elizabeth was born in the early hours of December 26 that year. It was 35 degrees below zero when she was born, and I had a new, warm winter coat wrapped up and waiting for Jim under the Christmas tree when I went into labor early Christmas morning. I gave it to him as he got ready to go out and warm up the car for our trip to the hospital, hoping to cheer him up. He'd had a series of serious medical problems as a child, and ever since had done everything he could to keep himself at a far distance from any medical establishment.

He was also worried about the house and our water pipes. We were heating the house solely with wood, and as full as he had stuffed the furnace, it would burn out eventually. The question was, how long would it take to have this baby? As things turned out it took a really long time, and Jim had to return home right after Elizabeth's birth to reload the furnace again.

We came home from the hospital on day five. It had been a challenging week for Jim with all the animals to feed, the furnace to keep going, and me and Elizabeth to visit in the hospital. It had been a challenging week for me, too. After many months of reading about pregnancy and childbirth, our LaMaze classes, and the excited anticipation, when it came right down to it and I went into labor, my doctor was off skiing somewhere in southern Vermont and we had to accept a substitute. And, after a twenty-six-hour labor, I was told that Elizabeth had to be born by caesarean section.

On New Year's Eve day, December 31, 1980, we were finally ready to go home: Elizabeth so tiny and dependent; Jim going through the motions of being responsible for getting us home safely to start our life as a family; and me: proud, sore, excited, and very nervous. I knew absolutely nothing about babies, had never even been particularly interested in them, and had no help to turn to. I was glad I'd have the rest of the semester break to figure things out.

I had made a good friend in law school who was living about fifteen minutes away from campus, and she invited me to stay with her during our last semester. I gratefully juggled my schedule and stayed with her two nights a week, utilizing a nearby babysitter during the day. Occasionally, as with my very late afternoon course in Family Law, or when I needed to have her close at hand in order to leave school promptly,

Elizabeth could be found in her infant seat under my desk, hopefully, but certainly not always, asleep.

Next on my to-do list after graduation was the bar exam. I found a woman who lived in Montpelier who was happy to look after Elizabeth while I attended the bar review course. I would get up early in the morning to get us both ready to travel, nurse her, drive to Montpelier and drop her off, attend the course for three hours, nurse her again before we left, and return to St. Johnsbury to study for the exam. My schedule was demanding, and I looked forward to the day when the bar exam would be over and I could take the time to get to know my daughter. But that proved to be a little too late. One day, while changing her on the bed, I looked away for a moment and she took that opportunity to turn over, rolling herself right off the bed and falling onto the floor, breaking her collar bone. I hadn't known she had learned to turn over!

My recurring nightmare at the time was that I would forget to pick Elizabeth up before leaving Montpelier, and would return to St. Johnsbury without her. It never actually happened, but the nightmare was bad enough that I decided I needed to find child care closer to home before I started my clerkship, although it would mean a longer day away from her. Luckily, I found a wonderful woman in Danville to care for her.

But even this child care arrangement was not without pitfalls. One spring morning during my clerkship, late in getting started out the door to Montpelier, I decided to take the back way to North Danville, which I thought would be quicker. We were in the midst of one of those spring snowstorms that can be heavy, though short lived. The road was thick with snow but manageable until I got to a point where it took a quick, steep dip. The wind had filled the dip with a large snowdrift, and before I could stop and back up my car, I found myself stuck in the dip, unable to go either forward or back.

I was dressed in my work clothes for court, and not a particularly heavy coat, but thankfully had boots on. Elizabeth was similarly underdressed since the forecast for the day had been that the snow would stop and give way to a beautiful warm sunny day. I hadn't planned on either of us being outside for more than the minute or two it took to get into the preheated car or make the stop in Danville.

Gauging our situation, I saw a farmhouse about a tenth of a mile away up the road and decided I could make it there with her, even having to carry her through the drifts; and really, I knew there wasn't much choice. This was long before cell phones, and the road was sparsely traveled at any time of day, let alone in the early morning in a snowstorm, so the chance of anyone coming by to assist us was pretty much nil.

I got an old army blanket out of the car and wrapped it around Elizabeth. I was only 5'½" tall, and with those especially short legs, it was slow going through the drifts as the snow continued to fall. It seemed like it took us forever to reach the house, but I could see lights on in the back, so I knew that people were home and likely awake; that was hopeful and kept me going.

When we got to the front door, I started ringing the bell and banging on the door as best I could with one hand. No response. Then I remembered that about a year and a half earlier an elderly brother and sister had been murdered in their home, which was the closest farmhouse to this one. These people must have been frightened for their lives hearing someone banging on their front door at such an unusual hour.

I looked into the blanket at Elizabeth, who had clammed right up as soon as I'd taken her out of the car and into the weather, and who had now shut down physically in all possible ways in an instinctive defense against the cold. I was getting pretty cold myself. Were we going to die here on the doorstep, I wondered, while the people inside hid from us in an effort to save themselves from a threat that didn't exist? It seemed a possibility.

After trying to raise someone for probably another minute or two, I decided there had to be another approach that would work and that Elizabeth was the key. Holding her tight to me, I made my way carefully through the even deeper snow under the edge of the roof along the side of the house until we came to the window of the room that was lit. I banged on the window with one fist and then held Elizabeth up with both hands, so that if they would even just take a peek outside they would see a baby. That did it! In no time we were inside with an elderly couple who fed and sheltered us most of the day until the snow plow showed up. They couldn't have been nicer, even tearing up some odd pieces of fabric they had to keep Elizabeth in dry diapers.

*   *   *

My year with Chief Justice Barney, "the Chief" as he was referred to at Court and within the Vermont bar, was an unforgettable experience. I have never thought of myself as an intellectual, but I spent that entire year delighting in one cerebral struggle after another in case after case. The Chief that year was the president of the American Association of Chief Justices, and that meant significant and time-consuming responsibilities over and above the already full schedule he had as a sitting justice and overseer of the entire Vermont judiciary. Because of this, he gave me a great deal of responsibility. Often I saw my draft opinions unchanged in any significant way prior to publication.

I loved the work. I loved working with the law, understanding how it had evolved on the issue that needed to be addressed, and sometimes taking it a step further to square with the facts of a case in a way that would achieve the result the justices desired as well as make sense to everyone who read the decision.

My enjoyment of my clerkship was also due in no small part to the collegial relationship that developed among the clerks. Although we came from different backgrounds and our ages spanned nearly fifteen years, we formed a very tight bond. This was particularly important to me and to my sense of professional well-being, since I saw so little of the Chief.

In celebration of our friendship, in the spring of our year together I organized a fishing trip on Lake Memphremagog to introduce my fellow clerks to the Northeast Kingdom and its pleasures. I invited all of the justices to join us, as well as retired Justice Rudolph Daley, whom we knew well as he had left the bench just a year before we arrived and frequently filled in when one of our "Js" had to recuse himself. As it turned out the only judge who accepted the invitation *was* Rudy Daley, who was from Newport, where our boat would launch. We sailed all day up to the Canadian border and back, as he regaled us with story after story about the Court, our "Js," and the Northeast Kingdom.

The outward atmosphere at the Court was appropriately serious and solemn. The courtroom itself featured a lot of dark paneled wood, dark green carpet, and well-shined brass. We clerks, who took turns in the courtroom filling water glasses, sharpening pencils, and explaining procedures to attorneys unfamiliar with the routine, were expected to dress professionally, which for me at that time meant in a dress and heels. It also meant dealing with the elite of Vermont's legal profession, and demanded a formality of behavior that I had not had to rise to before in Vermont.

As I got to know these attorneys from around the state, I began to realize that my clerkship was not only going to be a judicial learning experience for me, but also a networking opportunity that could help launch my career. My sense of identity as a Vermont attorney with something to say that people might listen to, and something to contribute that might benefit my adopted state, took root and began to grow. I was unsure at first exactly what form it would eventually take, but before I had finished my clerkship I had my first clue.

In 1981, when I had taken the bar exam, one of the graders had applied the grading scale backwards, affecting all of the papers he had graded and the overall grading curve. When the error was discovered everything had to be recalculated, and when it all became public, including Vermont's pass/fail statistics, there was a demand for a thorough look at Vermont's bar admission process, which typically resulted in a lower percentage of applicants being admitted each year than was the case in most other states. The result was the appointment of a commission chaired by former governor Phil Hoff, which would investigate the issues and make any necessary recommendations for change.

One of those who had failed the 1981 exam was a woman from Buffalo who had been part of our small bar review group in Montpelier, and with whom I had become friendly. After working for years as a paralegal for an attorney who had encouraged her to become an attorney herself, she had formalized her study of law and taken the Vermont bar exam along with the rest of us. When she learned she had failed the exam by only a few points she held her breath while the grades were recalculated, but again was told that she had failed. She then took the exam a second time, but failed again. She was a fine, intelligent, and compassionate person, and would have made a good attorney. But after being told three times that she was a failure, she went back to Buffalo. I felt terrible, and was moved to address the Hoff Commission.

When I appeared before the commission, I stated that my underlying premise was that the only acceptable purpose of requirements for admission to the bar ought to be the protection of the public, insofar as that is possible, by assuring that those who hold themselves out as lawyers are in fact competent to represent the interests of other people in and out of court, and of a character that will assure they do so with the highest of ethical standards. I rejected those aspects of the examination and the admission requirements that I felt went beyond that purpose in order to intentionally limit the number of attorneys admitted each year.

With the nontraditional lawyer explicitly in mind, I emphasized that a new generation of lawyers was coming to the law for reasons other than what had attracted students to the law in the past, and with new ideas about how they would integrate its practice into their lives. If the admission requirements were not amended to reflect this phenomenon, I said, Vermont was going to lose the services of many talented people. My comments were politely received.

The second indication of the role I might eventually play concerned Northeast Kingdom Community Action (NEKCA), the successor agency to OCCSA, the highly successful community action agency in the Northeast Kingdom that Jim had worked for until a political drama had sent the staff scattering and put its programs in peril.

The executive director of OCCSA, Tom Hahn, had proved himself a master at securing federal funding for a wide variety of programs, and the agency had for many years been overseeing everything from the distribution of garden seeds and surplus food to the construction of affordable housing with lumber cut and milled by the agency's CETA employees themselves. But Tom was a spirited character, and in spite of his success at building an agency that benefited so many low-income Vermonters, he had incurred the wrath of Governor Richard Snelling by referring to the governor as a "porky flatlander" when talking to a newspaper reporter, who promptly quoted him. The governor was incensed and set out to do Tom in.

Under the guise of "audit issues," the governor persuaded the federal Community Services Administration (CSA) to strip OCCSA of its administrative funding in 1980 and create a new agency to replace it, NEKCA. It was a nasty battle, which the governor ultimately won; but the OCCSA staff received considerable support, from the most humble of its low-income clients to the state's political elite. One champion was former Governor Tom Salmon, who, testifying on behalf of OCCSA at a defunding hearing held by CSA in January 1980 said, "[OCCSA] has done a damn good job fighting poverty in the Northeast Kingdom, Vermont's poorest region. . . anyone who thinks these have been routine investigations hasn't been reading the newspapers closely."[16]

The size, shape, and leadership of the new agency was still being determined in 1981-82 when I was clerking, and the essential questions were, what would it look like and who would run it? Would the remarkable effort Tom's staff had made on behalf of low-income Vermonters continue without Tom at the helm, or would the governor's personal vendetta destroy the effectiveness of the agency forever?

It was a very difficult time. Jim had taken the CETA program out of OCCSA as OCCSA slid into free fall, and was running it directly under the Vermont Department of Labor out of the old post office building in St. Johnsbury. But things were not going smoothly for the new agency, NEKCA, and the rest of the programs.

The first director selected to get the new agency off the ground had come from the Ford Foundation and left for greener pastures in a matter of months when the money he had expected did not come his way. The

------

[16] *Barre-Montpelier Times Argus,* January 25, 1980.

second director had to resign under pressure from the board after a period of employment that didn't last much longer than his predecessor's. At that point Jim threw his hat into the ring; but it was anybody's guess whether enough time had passed and enough dust had settled for someone so closely associated with Tom and OCCSA to be acceptable to the governor.

As I was preparing the courtroom one day during the NEKCA hiring process, in came John Dooley. I knew Dooley a bit from Vermont Legal Aid, where he had been the director when I interned there the summer before I entered law school. Now, at the governor's invitation, he was closely involved in shaping NEKCA's future. I knew him to be a compassionate person with a very keen mind who, if he wanted to, would certainly be able to sort out the mess that OCCSA and NEKCA had gone through and come up with the right answer.

There we were, alone in what may be the most somber room in the state of Vermont. In the midst of all that dark wood paneling and those heavy velvet drapes, I asked him if he "had a minute," and then unloaded on him nonstop my lengthy opinion of why it was time for the governor to let go of his anger at Tom and allow the dedicated staff from OCCSA to return to the agency and resume the good work they had been doing.

When the hiring process concluded, Jim had become the third director of NEKCA in less than three years, a job he held for nearly a decade. In his years at the helm he rebuilt the agency to a level where it employed 100 people and operated forty-five separate programs.

Toward the end of my clerkship, as I was wondering about my next step, Richard Axelrod from the St. Johnsbury law firm of Gensburg & Axelrod invited me to join the firm that he and Bob Gensburg had founded, to work primarily with him in his trial practice. It seemed a good idea at the time. Elizabeth would be just under two years old when I left the Court and I couldn't imagine working very far away from her. There was no labor law to be practiced on a regular basis in St. Johnsbury, which would have been my first choice, but Gensburg & Axelrod had an excellent reputation and I knew that the two partners shared my politics. I accepted the offer and learned a lot there, but lasted only a year due to the stress of the work coupled with demands at home. I left in 1983 to join the staff at the St. Johnsbury office of Vermont Legal Aid.

Working at Legal Aid was as comfortable as working at Gensburg & Axelrod had been stressful. We were a young and compatible staff, all committed to a social justice mission. Because our clientele was low income, much of the work was in the area of public benefits: unemployment compensation, food stamps, Medicaid, welfare, and Social Security, all programs I was familiar with from my former work as a social worker. I also served as the legal advisor to Umbrella, the local organization headquartered in the same building, that supported victims of domestic violence and sexual assault. I was doing important work, I felt good doing it, and it was compatible with new family responsibilities following the birth of our second child, Daniel, in the spring of 1984.

It was at Legal Aid that I first began doing Social Security disability work, specifically, helping low-income clients apply for Supplemental Security Income (SSI) benefits. As I began doing this work, I came to realize that virtually every applicant for SSI who believes he or she is unable to work is likely eligible for benefits under the Social Security regulations. These allow an administrative law judge to consider not only a claimant's medical issues, but also the context in which they exist: the claimant's age, education, and work history, and how the overall effect of these factors determines their ability to hold a job.

Telling that story to a judge is not a simple matter. Reading through reams of medical records in order to find the kernels of information that will make a difference, being able to draft clear and convincing letters for busy physicians to approve and sign, and ferreting out evidence of the pertinent nonmedical factors that will lead to a favorable decision often requires a great amount of work. Many of the claimants I worked with had dropped out of schools or worked for employers that hadn't kept good records, and in many cases no longer existed. Reconstructing a client's personal history was a very time-consuming challenge.

Since an attorney's payment for SSI work depends on the size of the past-due award the claimant eventually receives, rather than how many hours it takes an attorney to secure it, most private attorneys can't earn the money they want to make representing low-income claimants whose potential awards are going to be quite small. Therefore, they don't take their cases, leaving them without the professional help they need to succeed. I felt called upon to fill this gap, and would continue to do this work for most of the next thirty years, regardless of whatever else I might be doing or who I might be working for. I never bothered to figure out how much I earned on an hourly basis from my SSI work because I didn't want to know. I comforted myself instead with my success rate and the thank yous I received from grateful claimants and their physicians.

Over the years I also developed a specialty representing Social Security disability claimants with multiple chemical sensitivity (MCS). MCS was not even recognized by the Social Security Administration as a legitimate medical condition when I began. But the challenge of successfully making the case for a close friend who had been chemically injured by materials used in the construction of a new courthouse where she had gone to work as an assistant court clerk, and for the child of another friend, who needed special education accommodations after being chemically injured by a newly carpeted kindergarten room, opened my eyes to the tremendous need for help among the MCS population.

Word soon spread in the MCS community of my willingness to take on these cases that were medically very difficult to prove and subject to the skepticism of just about everyone involved in the process. Soon I was travelling a good portion of the state to meet with potential clients in their homes, one of the few places in which their safety could be assured. Many of these clients had good work histories prior to being chemically injured, and so were eligible for benefits on which they would be able to manage financially. I was pleased to be able to help make this happen.

Vermont Law School graduation, May, 1981, with Elizabeth

(top left) Mother's Day Peace Rally, with Elizabeth, May, 1981

(top right) March for Women's Equality/Women's Lives, Washington D.C., 1986, with Sheila Reed

(bottom left) Campaigning with Elizabeth and Daniel, 1988

Chapter Nine

Into the Fray

The 1980s

The birth of my children, just as I was reentering the workforce as an attorney, brought home to me the importance of family-friendly policies for parents and children. This would be at the core of much of my legal and political work for the rest of my life.

I was fortunate that in late 1980, when Elizabeth was born, the women's movement was at its height. Any conference or major meeting I went to during my last semester of law school and for quite a few years after that, offered free, high-quality child care.

I first brought Elizabeth, and then Elizabeth and Daniel, to many of these conferences and meetings, happily and without guilt. When one or the other was nursing, or when Jim was not available, the only other choice would have been to stay home. Unfortunately, this focus on affordable child care as an essential benefit for working parents has lost its edge today as legislators and governors with other priorities have come to dominate their states.

In 1981 friends in the Newport area organized a Mother's Day rally in response to an attempt by Representative Henry Hyde and Senator Jesse Helms to restrict the right to an abortion through congressional action. The organizers asked me to speak, and with someone holding five-month-old Elizabeth nearby, I addressed the many issues confronting working women, including the critical need for family planning services and reproductive choice, the need for mothers who work as homemakers or domestic help to be able to access Social Security and unemployment benefits, and the right to safe and healthy workplaces and equal pay.

In March 1983 the Vermont Governor's Commission on Women held hearings around the state on the challenges facing working mothers, and I testified to my personal experience, laying it out as plainly as I could. I ended with the story of my departure from Gensburg & Axelrod, which had been precipitated by my request for a four-day work week. After lengthy deliberation, to the partners' credit they agreed. But in doing so they left me with two unforgettable statements: First, that I couldn't be a good lawyer if I only worked part time; and second, that unless I returned to full-time work I would never be a partner in the firm.

Those two statements were totally out of touch with the reality of working mothers. Most women today, like most men, work to survive. And as long as working women are also going to be responsible for bearing and raising our children, we are going to have to address their needs by making very basic changes. The partners weren't ready for me. I gave my notice and went to work for Legal Aid. When Daniel was born a year later, I was grateful that Legal Aid allowed me to install a crib for him in my office, where he happily hung out until he was six months old. I appreciated just how lucky I was and felt it an important enough area of concern to raise my voice for others in the same situation.

I was on a roll. Less than two months after my appearance before the Governor's Commission, I accepted a friend's invitation to speak on behalf of a Newport-based peace committee at another Mother's Day event, and three months after that I returned to my very favorite topic with an op-ed column in the local newspaper titled, "What About Baby? The Case for Employer Sponsored Child Care." I reviewed the historic treatment of child care as an employee benefit, as employers became aware that the presence or absence of adequate, affordable child care in a community affects employee morale, productivity, absenteeism, and turnover rates. I discussed what companies taking the lead in Vermont were doing about it, hoping to raise awareness of the benefits of the new Economic Recovery Act of 1981 among both employers and employees.

I was happy to be able to address women's employment issues as well through my legal work at Legal Aid. One case I was proud of was *Shufelt v. Department of Employment and Training.*[17] At issue was whether parental demands could constitute good cause for refusing work while receiving unemployment benefits. Ms. Shufelt's ex-husband was stalking her house and because of this she could not find a babysitter willing to care for her children at night in order to take the second-shift job that was offered. When she declined the offer, the state terminated her unemployment benefits.

In analyzing case precedent and statutory authority for the Vermont Supreme Court appeal, I determined that a prior Supreme Court case, cited as precedent for twenty years, had been decided in error based on a misinterpretation of statutory law. My brief, and the oral argument of the attorney who succeeded me at Legal Aid, Sheila Reed, persuaded the Court to overturn its earlier holding and reach a favorable decision in our case. The case is now included in a family law textbook.[18]

While at Legal Aid I was given time off to serve as an American Civil Liberties Union cooperating attorney in *Doe v. Celani,*[19] a landmark class action that overturned the state's prohibition on Medicaid payment for medically necessary abortions. "Jane Doe" was a low-income mother

---

[17] 531 A.2d 894 (1987).
[18] Richard McHugh and Ingrid Koch, "Unemployment Insurance: Responding to the Expanding Role of Women in the Work Force," *Clearinghouse Review* (April 1994): 1425, note 33.
[19] No. S81-84CnC (slip op.) (Vt. Super. Ct., May 26, 1986).

on Medicaid, with just one remaining kidney due to a childhood illness, and that one a transplant. She became unintentionally pregnant while in the process of arranging to undergo sterilization, which her physicians had recommended to protect her from serious medical complications that would likely occur should she become pregnant again. Although loss of kidney function would not have resulted in death—a situation that would have triggered Medicaid payment for an abortion under the terms of the Hyde Amendment—it would have forced her back on dialysis. Several health organizations had refused to perform an abortion without payment, and the Vermont Department of Social Welfare had turned down her request for Medicaid funding.

Attorney Bill Dorsch and I took the case to court in January 1984, and obtained an injunction requiring the department to pay for Jane's abortion, as well as a broader ruling requiring Medicaid payment for any such medically necessary abortions in the future. At the direction of Governor Kunin the State did not appeal the decision, and Medicaid payment for medically necessary abortions remains the law in Vermont to this day, one of only sixteen states in which that is true.

I had joined the Vermont Bar Association in 1982 and had been making a name for myself in other ways. When Vermont's Abuse Prevention Act was passed by the legislature in 1981, I had served as co-author and editor, with Amy Davenport and Jeri Martinez, of "Abuse Prevention," a training manual prepared for use by private attorneys in the Vermont Volunteer Lawyers Project.

My public exposure then increased exponentially in 1983-84, when I was asked to chair a special bar association committee on judicial selection criteria in the midst of a controversy concerning the fairness of Vermont's judicial selection process, which had failed to produce a single woman judge.

The committee was charged to review current procedures, recommend changes, and identify appropriate selection criteria. We worked diligently, interviewing everyone involved in the process from the Judicial Nominating Board to the chief justice and the governor, and sifting through volumes of information from other states. We released our report in April 1984, accompanied by a strong statement authored by me, in which we criticized the Judicial Nominating Board for overstepping its limited authority to weed out unqualified applicants and forward the names of all other applicants to the governor. Instead, we concluded, the board had been selecting from the pool of qualified applicants only those few individuals it deemed best suited to fill the vacancies, all of whom had been men, thus inappropriately sharing the governor's power to appoint judges without also sharing his or her public accountability.

The board reacted angrily to the criticism and the controversy was greeted with front-page headlines across the state. Daniel figured amusingly in my activities: I had given birth to him the night before the report was officially released, and was hospitalized and unavailable for comment when the Judicial Selection Board's response to our statement hit the papers. In the end, to the committee's great credit, the Vermont Legislature adopted verbatim the selection criteria we had developed, and codified them into law at 4 V.S.A. s.602(d).

When the furor died down I was encouraged to run for the Judicial Nominating Board myself and was extremely proud of the support I garnered from the Northern District, including Burlington, whose representative I would be if elected. A letter on my behalf signed by four highly respected attorneys was sent to every lawyer in the district, describing the work I and five other women attorneys had done on the Judicial Selection Committee, and crediting us with bringing "the all-male composition of the VT judiciary to the attention of the public—and keeping it there—until things changed."[20] With support like that it was no wonder I was elected, but I declined the position in order to accept one even nearer and dearer to my heart that came in the midst of the election: appointment by Governor Kunin to the Vermont Labor Relations Board.

Were the Judicial Nominating Board and Labor Board positions exclusive? No, and I felt badly at declining the Judicial Nominating Board position after so many people, and in particular the four attorneys who endorsed me, had gone to such lengths to show their support. But there was a limit to what I could take on, and I felt I had already made a major contribution to the matter of selecting judges in Vermont. The Labor Board appointment was my dream: a quasi-judicial position in the field of labor law. I couldn't pass up the opportunity and accepted the appointment in February 1987.

Clearly, the decade of the 1980s since my admission to the bar and clerkship had been overloaded professionally for me. In addition to the VBA Committee on Judicial Selection Criteria and the Vermont Labor Relations Board, I was appointed to the Vermont State Advisory Committee of the U.S. Commission on Civil Rights in 1983, elected a member of the VBA's Board of Bar Managers in 1984, appointed an associate member of the Board of Bar Examiners in 1985, and also became chair of the Task Force on Domestic Violence of the Governor's Commission on Women in 1985, co-authoring with Kathy Johnson the Task Force report "Abuse Prevention and the Criminal Justice System," which was released in late 1986. In 1988 I was appointed to the Vermont Task Force on Gender Bias in the Legal System.

Although the Task Force positions were designed to be of limited duration and I saw them through, my tenure on the standing committees

---

[20] Letter from Ritchie Berger, Robert Gensburg, Christopher Davis, and David Wilson to Northern District attorneys, November 24, 1986.

and boards to which I'd been elected or appointed was sometimes brief. I had a baby and a toddler who needed me, and they came first. Jim did what he could, but he was commuting nearly an hour each way to Newport every day, and with the evening meetings he had to attend had limited time to give.

*   *   *

While I was still at Legal Aid, my friend and former colleague from our days together as Supreme Court law clerks, Michael Marks, began trying to recruit me to work for the Vermont Department of Public Service, where he had become Vermont's public advocate. I was flattered, but resisted. For one thing, I was happy where I was at Legal Aid. In addition, working full time with two children under five was not an easy matter, and I had no desire to make my life even more stressful and complicated by having to commute to Montpelier and learn an entirely new field of law. Utility regulation had never been a particular interest of mine, and certainly wasn't an area of expertise, so it was a bit of a mystery why Michael was so persistent, but persistent he was. When the offer finally became defined as a part-time job that would require a commute just three days a week but would still pay me what I needed to bring in, I finally said yes.

I started at the Public Service Department in 1985 and at first my assignments were all over the place. There seemed to be no focus to what I was doing, nor a particular area of work that I was needed for. I got to know the rest of the staff and a little bit about what they each did, but the feeling of mystery about what I was doing there stayed with me until Michael finally put an end to it.

I had been hired to analyze the legality of contracts for nuclear power from the Seabrook nuclear facility that six Vermont municipalities and a Vermont cooperative had entered into some years before with a Massachusetts power wholesaler. Michael and Public Service Commissioner Jerry Tarrant wanted to see what I thought about the legality of the contracts. With that I commenced nearly three years of work as a Department of Public Service attorney and special assistant attorney general on the most challenging case of my legal career, *Vermont Department of Public Service v. Massachusetts Municipal Wholesale Electric Company, et al.*[21]

In retrospect, I can understand why Michael recruited me for this task. After working together for a year at the Supreme Court, no one knew more about my research ability, my writing style, or my work ethic than my fellow clerks, and Michael was the one I had been closest to. Clearly, he had a view of my work that was compatible with the needs of the case.

The fact is that my most important and successful legal work has turned on excruciatingly close and extensive reading of statutes, legislative history, municipal contracts, and other documents, and on my ability to persuasively discuss their relevance to the issue at hand. I had once asked Justice Franklin Billings, who became chief justice the year after my clerkship, for a reference, and he had referred to me in his letter of recommendation as an "excellent technician." I was a bit insulted by this label at the time, and would have preferred to have been referred to as an "excellent analyst" or "insightful" or something on that order, but over the years I have come to accept his words as an accurate professional compliment.

In the *MMWEC* case the causes of action were complex, and in very important ways novel. The initial complaint ran to thirty-three pages, and between that complaint and the final Vermont Supreme Court ruling, thirty-two other pleadings were involved, culminating in plaintiffs' 170-page Joint Memorandum in Support of Summary Judgment. Records had to be combed through in each of the municipal offices, statutory law researched and interpreted, and cases from other jurisdictions carefully analyzed for their value

---

[21]558 A.2d 215 (1988).

as precedent. In recruiting me for the job, Michael correctly anticipated the extent and nature of the work that would be involved.

After the trial court ruled against us, Jerry, Michael, and I were called over to the governor's office to meet with Governor Kunin and her legal counsel, John Dooley, to discuss the trial court's decision and whether that ruling should be appealed. Many of the issues involved were issues of first impression in Vermont, and there had been little clear precedent from other jurisdictions.

I knew both Kunin and Dooley by this time, but had never had to give legal advice to such high-ranking individuals, and in this case there were significant political aspects to be considered as well. The State had sued five of its own municipalities and a Vermont electric co-op in addition to the Massachusetts entity, and millions of dollars in future rate payments by Vermont consumers were at stake. In addition, the opinions of some of Vermont's most prominent utility lawyers, who had advised the municipalities and the co-op that the contracts were legal, were being called into question. All this put the governor's reputation and that of her legal counsel squarely on the line. I said relatively little at the meeting, letting Michael and Jerry do most of the talking on our side of the table.

After the meeting Michael and Jerry went on ahead, the governor's staff disappeared, and I made a stop in the ladies' room. I emerged just in time to catch the 5th-floor elevator door before it closed, realizing as I hastily stepped in that the only other passengers were Governor Kunin and her bodyguard. The governor spoke first.

"Dinah," she asked, looking me straight in the eye, "are we going to win this appeal?" That was really the question we'd all been skirting for about the past hour.

"Yes," I said, returning her direct gaze, and added, "I'm quite sure of it," hoping fervently I was right. As it turned out I was, and we were able to save Vermont ratepayers $327 million dollars.

*   *   *

As my *MMWEC* work was winding down, the effort to pass a Vermont Equal Rights Amendment was just ramping up. Vermont had been the first state to ratify the federal ERA in 1973, and had staunchly adhered to that position ever since. But the federal effort had been defeated, leading Governor Snelling to ask the Governor's Commission on Women in 1982 to research the question of whether Vermont should amend its own state constitution to include a state ERA. The answer was "yes."

As was constitutionally required, the state ERA was put to a vote in two separately elected bienniums of the Vermont Legislature in 1983 and 1985. It passed both times by large margins. The next and final hurdle was a required public referendum, which was scheduled for November 4, 1986. While a successful result seemed likely, given the history, it was not a foregone conclusion; nine states had lost state ERA campaigns since 1973 despite equally encouraging early polls, after significant infusions of money from right-wing political action groups and emotionally charged advertising campaigns.

I jumped into the fray early on with Elizabeth, then four, taking her with me as "Exhibit A" to testify before the House Judiciary Committee in 1985 when it considered the amendment. My involvement in the campaign continued at a high pace. I was appointed chair of the Caledonia County Committee for the ERA and we ran a vigorous campaign.

Women came out of the woodwork to form teams of door-to-door canvassers who spent their Saturdays blanketing every town and hamlet in Caledonia and southern Essex counties with ERA literature, until we couldn't think of another place to canvass. Under the guidance of a local journalist, Chris Camara, we made a documentary film for public-access TV that consisted of interviews with local women talking about why they supported the Amendment. It ran repeatedly. Five hundred women and men of every political persuasion came forward to support the ERA and lend their names to a two-page endorsement spread in the *Caledonian-Record*.

Although already known as a progressive state, at the time Vermont lacked laws prohibiting discrimination based on sex in commercial lending, education, employment, and pay. But either the people of Vermont weren't listening, or they didn't care. When it came time to vote, the Vermont ERA went down to defeat.

Still, our efforts did not come to nothing. Out of our county campaign was born the Caledonia County Women's Network. Gov. Kunin kicked off the Network's organizing effort with an address to 126 area women at the Lincoln Inn on February 9, 1987. Shortly thereafter, I'm sure in large part because of my ERA campaign leadership and my role as a cofounder of the Women's Network, I was honored by Umbrella as a recipient of one of its first "Wonder Woman" awards "for raising the quality of life for other women in the community."

*   *   *

As my work on *MMWEC* drew to a close, I also opened my own law office in St. Johnsbury, primarily taking family and administrative law cases. Right off the bat I found myself representing the plaintiff in the first challenge to the state's new child support guidelines. I had known her for many years before she brought me a motion for modification of child support filed by her ex-husband, based on his remarriage and new responsibility to support his second wife and her child from a previous relationship. The issue was whether expenses for a second wife and stepchild should enter into the calculation of child support owed to a preexisting family. The case went up to the Vermont Supreme Court, which supported our position that those circumstances should not be considered, then settled after remand based on that decision.

The cases I got most passionate about in my new practice were the ones that paid the least, where under a contract with the defender general's office I represented parents and occasionally children in cases brought by the State alleging child abuse or neglect. In some of these cases the evidence was heavily against my clients and the charges were clearly warranted; I had to advise the parents that the State was likely to have no difficulty proving its case; unless the parents wanted to fight the inevitable, their best use of me was to advocate for a plan that would lead to reunification of the family as quickly as possible.

In other cases, however, it was far less clear whether the parents were truly guilty of abuse or neglect, or were simply not raising their children in a manner the State would prefer. The imbalance of power in these cases, which pitted the values of middle-class social workers against the efforts of well-meaning parents struggling to raise their children in poverty, was almost insurmountable, but it was my job to try.

I also continued to serve on the Labor Relations Board throughout the period of my private practice. I was in seventh heaven with my work there: once again intellectually immersed in labor law as well as serving in a quasi-judicial capacity, hearing cases involving municipal and nonprofit employees as well as employees of the State of Vermont, and working with four fine and thoughtful fellow Board members. We didn't always agree, of course, but we shared a mutual respect for each other and had an easy and productive working relationship.

But financing a law office was a struggle given my many low-income clients, and litigation was definitely not my forte. Standing up and speaking authoritatively to a judge and responding to questions as if I had all the answers was contrary to my nature. I was also constantly afraid of being unprepared in court. When a police officer came to my office at 2 am one night to see if a burglary was in progress, only to find me preparing for my appearance in a rather routine case I had the next day, I knew that something was very wrong and that a drastic change had to be made. So, in 1988, when Governor Kunin called to ask me to run for the legislature, she didn't have to do a lot of convincing.

Running my own campaign was something I'd long wanted to do. I felt I knew my community well, and that my political priorities were a good match for the social and economic needs of the people who lived in it. Although no Democrat had dared to run in St. Johnsbury for the past eight years and I doubted that I, as a relative newcomer, would be the one to do it successfully, I knew that my main reason for running—to give people a choice—would result in a campaign that was truly a group effort. I looked forward to campaigning and seeing how my ideas would be received.

My announcement was a lengthy introduction of me and my qualifications in the *Caledonian-Record*, which ran it front and center on page 1. My campaign literature stressed that I was "able to listen, willing to act," and that as the district's representative I'd be "asking the right questions, getting the right answers." Letters were drafted for volunteers to sign and send to friends and relatives who lived in the district, making my case and encouraging them to support me; well-known residents of St. Johnsbury appeared in individual newspaper endorsements next to their picture and were interviewed on the local radio station; buttons and bumper stickers were designed and distributed; reminder postcards were sent and reminder phone calls were made. I knew it had been a well-designed campaign when even the *Caledonian-Record*, in its pre-election day editorial, said I'd been "making a particularly favorable impression" on the campaign trail, before endorsing my opponents.[22] Unfortunately, I was soundly beaten.

After the election, when it was definite that the legislature wasn't going to occupy my time, I needed to find something else to do again. Fortuitously, it was at that moment that the St. Johnsbury regional coordinator for the Agency of Human Services decided to resign, and after a slight delay caused by the legislature's ambivalence over whether to continue funding the positions, by mid-March 1989 I was the new AHS regional coordinator in St. Johnsbury.

---

[22] *Caledonian-Record*, October 28, 1988, 4.

The position was another good fit. During the fifteen years that had elapsed since the state had created the Agency of Human Services in the early 1970s, the proliferation of nonprofit service providers had continued apace. The regional resource groups that I had begun in Newport when I was the resource coordinator there were still performing an important communication and networking function for direct service providers, but it was now also necessary to try to coordinate things at an administrative and policymaking level to avoid duplication of services and inconsistent outcomes.

I'd had previous experience with many of the people I was now working with again, and had remained in touch with some of them over the years. Several were now managers of their respective departments, others had moved outside the agency and were at a management level in the private nonprofits. I was happy to have a history with them on which I could build. Of course, the nonprofit providers were under no obligation to buy into the new effort at regional coordination, but many recognized both the need for coordination and the advantage to having an advocate within the state system, which both funded and regulated much of what they did.

That said, even those who had created the new positions weren't quite sure what result they wanted. The positions were controversial not only with legislators, whose limited knowledge of social services hampered their understanding of the problem and caused them to question the price tag for solving it, but with many of the AHS managers as well, who feared that their relative autonomy was being reined in. Most of them were happy to request funds for special projects or my endorsement of their new ideas, but were reluctant to accept coordination of their work with that of their colleagues, public or private. About the only thing the various players could be counted on to agree about was that I was the one who was responsible for the building, from auditing compliance with handicapped access regulations to ordering toilet paper.

Then, suddenly one night, the state office building we all shared burned to the ground. In a matter of hours the disaster displaced over fifty state workers in six different departments and destroyed thousands of client files, court records, and many years of professional work. It also left our clients, particularly those least able to cope on their own, with nowhere to turn for assistance in accessing the services and benefits they relied on to deal with their own emergencies.

It fell to me to take control of a very emotional and chaotic situation, to set priorities and enforce them, yet to deal patiently, courteously, and tactfully with the many distraught individuals who had questions. The managers all rose to the occasion and made a remarkably quick recovery as we all set aside our suddenly insignificant differences and worked together for the benefit of our clients.

Within forty-eight hours the agency was functioning again out of a nearby motel. Over the next six months, thanks to excellent communication between and among department heads, it continued to function smoothly through two subsequent moves until we all came to rest again in the rebuilt state office building.

*   *   *

Meanwhile, however, all was not well with me personally. In February, during one of my routine examinations for breast cancer, I was found to have increased breast calcifications as well as atypical ductal hyperplasia, both conditions thought to often precede the disease. I had tremendous trust in my physician, a breast cancer specialist whom I had been seeing for years, but who, with these new developments, was estimating my chance of developing breast cancer before age 50 to be around 80 percent.

When I asked him point blank what I should do, he said I had two choices: continued careful observation or bilateral mastectomies, which, if all breast tissue was successfully removed, would provide total protection for the rest of my life. There was no middle ground. I did not *have* breast cancer, so there was no cancer treatment indicated. The conditions I did have were not in and of themselves going to affect me adversely, so there was nothing that needed to be done about *them*. If I chose continued close observation, all I could do was hope I didn't develop breast cancer, or if I did, that it would be treated successfully. There was no rush to decide what to do, he said; I should take my time and think it over.

I decided to get second and third opinions, and was referred to another breast cancer specialist at Massachusetts General Hospital, and to Dr. Susan Love, then at the Dana-Farber Cancer Institute. The opinion of the Mass General physician was more encouraging, putting my risk at 30 percent, but several of his comments made it clear to me that he hadn't read my file as carefully as I felt he should have, so I was left with little confidence in his opinion after traveling all the way to Boston to get it.

That left Susan Love and another trip to Boston. After spending considerable time educating me about the various stages of breast cancer as they were understood at the time, she put my risk of developing breast cancer within 25 years at 40 percent, which she considered a very high risk. Love also said she couldn't reassure me that careful observation would catch any cancer that did develop in time to assure recovery. Little real progress had been made in treatment, she said, and some breast cancers were so aggressive that they could never be successfully treated no matter how early they were identified, at least not by current means. It was her view that prophylactic mastectomies were the only thing that could guarantee survival, and while it might be overkill, anything less was nonexistent.

Having the ear of an expert who was also a woman, I asked Love what she would do if she were in my position. Her answer was that she would have the surgery, although she was honest enough to say that she couldn't guarantee that when actually faced with the decision for herself there wouldn't be psychological or emotional factors that might intervene and change her mind. That was enough for me. I returned to Vermont and scheduled the surgery for May, exactly twenty years to the month after my mother's death from the disease.

The next step was to prepare the kids. One cool spring evening when we had a nice fire going in the fireplace and all seemed right with the world, Jim and I gathered the kids in the living room and explained the situation. I told them that my breasts had gotten sick, and to make sure that they didn't make the rest of me sick, I was going to have them taken off. I said I'd have to go away for a night or two to do this, but that their father would be staying with them while Uncle Peter kept me company while I was away. Daniel, 5, giggled; Elizabeth, 8, seemed to accept the news as a matter of fact and nothing to get alarmed about.

The surgery went well and the next morning I was feeling good physically and mentally. My last words before I had gone under the anesthesia had been to say silently to my mother and my friend Jane Bayer that I was doing this for them, because I knew they would certainly have taken this option had they had the chance. When I awoke, I had no regrets about my decision and the fact of being breastless seemed rather inconsequential, as it has ever since.

As I lay in the hospital bed waiting to be discharged, I wondered why I had always heard that mastectomies were so emotionally traumatic for women. Even allowing for some variation in how attached women are to their breasts and how much a woman's personal identity can be based on her body image, it seemed highly unlikely that I was so psychologically different from every other woman who had gone through this surgery as to account for my very different reaction.

The only difference between me and other women I'd known or heard about who had had a mastectomy was that I didn't have cancer. I could only conclude that women who did have cancer came out of their mastectomies converting their fear of cancer and an untimely death into anger at being disfigured and anxiety that they would no longer be admired as women.

When I reached this conclusion it made a lot of sense to me. I think many people interpret fear as weakness, and it's a rare person who is able to talk about the possibility of her own death. But by converting those emotions into something more acceptable to feel and discuss, women who undergo mastectomies for breast cancer make it possible to communicate about their situation with family and friends and get the emotional support they need. I, on the other hand, having been spared the cancer diagnosis, was also spared the fear and anger. What I was left with was relief that the surgery was over and that I didn't have to worry about dying of breast cancer every day for the rest of my life.

I was and remain very grateful for my outcome, but I have also always felt guilty about it, that I got off so easily. And I feel guilty every time another friend or relative is diagnosed. A childhood friend whose virulent strain of breast cancer was in remission when she visited me, but was almost certain to return, said to me, "Boy, I'll bet you're sure glad you had those prophylactic mastectomies!" I am, and I miss her.

I was discharged the day after the surgery with a prescription for painkillers. Peter and I stopped at Ben & Jerry's in Waterbury on the way home for ice cream cones, and as I was in no pain and feeling good in general, I threw my prescription away in the Ben & Jerry's trash can. Big mistake. Shortly after arriving home the painkillers I'd been given that morning wore off, and I was hurting bad. Sheepishly I called my physician and explained my stupidity. A new prescription was called in.

The following day was a beautiful May day, and the sun was shining strongly enough to warm things up. I decided to convalesce on our deck, but as I changed from my nightgown into clothes for the day I was brought up short with a new thought: Now that I have no breasts, do I have to wear a top? Men don't have to wear tops, and the only difference seems to be that they don't have sex organs that need to be hidden from public view. So I didn't think so, and went out on the deck wearing just a pair of shorts.

My attitude made sense for a day or two, but seemed to make everyone else uncomfortable, so I quickly gave up this new freedom in favor of convention and returned to wearing tops. It didn't take long for me to return to conventional feelings about being covered up as well.

Unfortunately, breast cancer continued to be a part of my life through the illnesses and often deaths of far too many friends and relatives. Five years after my own surgery, I decided to honor the personal struggles of my mother and Jane, who had fought to the bitter end not to depart this earth prematurely, leaving children behind whose futures they would never know. Both women had been social workers, and both were strong believers in the importance of accurate information as a critical first step in problem solving and decision making. Establishing a place where area women would have easy access to current and comprehensive information about the prevention and treatment of breast cancer, as well as to the personal stories of women who had survived, seemed a fitting and useful way to honor them. I established the St. Johnsbury Athenaeum Breast Cancer Resource Library and donations poured in, more than doubling my goal. The library quickly became a reality.

Building "Kids Park and Seniors Too,"
Lincoln City, Oregon 1992

Chapter Ten

The Bingo Wars

1990-1993

I n 1990 we moved to Oregon. Many people thought the move was motivated by my defeat in the 1988 legislative race, a rejection, if you will, of a town that had rejected me. This was not the case. Nor did we move out of embarrassment, as my stepdaughter believed, after her friend published in *Vermont Woman* a not-too-thinly-disguised account of my prophylactic mastectomies, and the entire community—or so it felt—started staring at my chest. The truth was that there were two very different reasons for the move: one professional, that made me despair of ever having the judicial career I wanted; the other very personal.

The Vermont Legislature had recently created two new judgeships. Having discovered during law school and my judicial clerkship how much I enjoyed the intellectual challenge of being on the decision-making end of things, I badly wanted to fill one of the new positions. I also felt that given my work to open up the Vermont judiciary to women, my quasi-judicial experience on the Vermont Labor Relations Board, and the ongoing support I had received from Governor Kunin in several endeavors, it was possible she would appoint me if I made it through the nominating process while she was still in office.

I went to my interview with the Judicial Nominating Board not confident, but hopeful. All went predictably well for a while, but this was just a little over two years since Ronald Reagan's nomination of Douglas Ginsburg to the United States Supreme Court had fallen apart when Ginsburg's use of marijuana, while a Harvard professor, became public. In retrospect, I suppose I should have had Ginsburg's fate in mind, but when Board Chairman Philip Hoff asked me about past marijuana use I was not expecting it, and not being a quick thinker I did not have a good answer ready, so I simply gave the honest one, which was "yes."

Hoff may just have wanted everyone in the room to be sure how *he* felt about drug use, but when he went into what seemed like a rant in response to my answer, not only was my hope of having my name be passed on to the governor dashed, but he completely humiliated me in front of some of the most influential people in the Vermont bar. I left the interview quite sure that the career I wanted was no longer available to me.

I had to do some serious thinking about the future. I had been increasingly missing my extended family ever since I'd had kids, and the cancer forecast had given me further pause. Jim and I were no youngsters, and our two young children had no living grandparents and barely knew their relatives on my side of the family, nearly all of whom lived on the West Coast.

My father's death in January 1990 put an end to my need to be in Vermont to oversee his care, and had started me thinking about ways I might bring the kids closer to my family. The most obvious way was to bring them physically closer, by moving west. I'd put it out of my mind in favor of applying for one of the new judgeships, but now it seemed there was no longer any reason not to move.

Although my father had not been able to communicate or interact at all for quite a long while prior to his death, I had continued to visit him on a regular basis, often with the kids in tow. I always felt that until the medical community could definitively say that Alzheimer's victims could not understand what was being said to them, I had to assume that my father *could* understand me, and I related to him on that basis, even though he never responded in any way. The finality of his death had been a significant blow, no doubt exacerbated by the guilt I felt at having been the one who made the final decision to place him in a nursing home rather than keep trying to find a way to care for him in our home.

When his death finally came, I felt I owed it to him to be the one who took him back out of the nursing home. So, after the staff had kindly cleaned him up and gently wrapped him in a blanket, we carefully lifted him onto the back seat of my car in a sitting position, and I very carefully drove the thirty miles back to St. Johnsbury, and the funeral home that would handle his further arrangements. It was snowing, and I'd been reminded before I left that if I went off the road, I'd have a lot of explaining to do.

As I drove, I talked to him. I thanked him for all he'd done for me throughout my life, and for all the hard work he'd put in so that I could have the advantages I'd enjoyed. I recalled the fun times we'd had through the years doing things together, and apologized for not having been able to care for him myself during his final illness. I told him how much I loved him, and said my final goodbye. Taking that last trip with him was one of the best things I've ever done.

*   *   *

I chose Oregon as the best place for us to head, being the less expensive alternative to California. Jim, ever resistant to change of any kind, was not pleased and said he wouldn't go. I said the rest of us were going anyway, and began to make plans. Faced with the possible disappearance of his family, he slowly came around.

In the early summer I flew out to Portland to find us a place to live. I have always liked Portland, and in 1990 it was already well on its way to being the happening place it is today. I'm an easy nester, and I was confident that in a city that size, with many attractive neighborhoods, I could easily find a place for us in a week to ten days.

I went to work immediately upon my arrival. But every time I found a house I felt would be good for us, my cousin, with whom I was staying, would comment about the crime rate in that neighborhood, or the bad schools, or something equally disqualifying. I was working hard to find us a place to live, but she wasn't making it easy.

After four solid days of this I decided to take a day off from my house hunt and go to the coast for a break. A friend in St. Johnsbury had asked me to check on a house that she and her husband still owned in Lincoln City, if I had the time. They had decided to sell it after renting it for many years, but the realtor who managed it was telling them it wasn't worth what they hoped to get for it. I called the realtor and arranged to see it.

I had never lived by an ocean or any other large body of water, and the Oregon coast is one of the most spectacular stretches of oceanfront in the country. I left Portland early enough in the day to spend most of the morning driving along the shoreline with my mouth agape at the huge waves and tall rock formations not far from shore, stopping now and then to walk along the beach, which in Oregon is publicly owned.

I met Smokey Aschenbrenner in the afternoon, and he took me to the house. It was a small, older, two-story house just a stone's throw from Siletz Bay at the south end of Lincoln City. The house sat perched on a knoll with a curving stone stairway up to the front door, and was unlike any of the surrounding homes, which were mostly tiny cottages built in the 1930s as vacation rentals.

Smokey was a font of information and told me that the neighborhood was called Cutler City, the name a vestige of its former independent status. It was located at the southern end of what became Lincoln City in late 1964 when five small towns merged. Cutler City had always been known as a workingman's town, a popular tent city for tourists of modest means in the 1920s. Gradually the tents had been replaced by the little cottages, which were just now starting to be replaced by large vacation homes along the water's edge.

The area had thick vegetation made up in no small part of beautiful wild rhododendrons, which were in full bloom. There was something very appealing about the little neighborhood, not least of which was the history visible in its architecture, and the diversity of inhabitants it suggested. It occupied a small peninsula bounded on three sides by the bay, and on the fourth side by highway 101, which runs up the Pacific coast from Southern California to the Canadian border.

The house itself was indeed the worse for wear after many rentals, the last by a motorcycle gang, who had left it in tatters. But I fell in love with it and with the neighborhood, and after a call to Jim, pretty much on impulse decided to buy it. In the process of all this, Smokey and I got pretty chatty, and as the deal closed he asked me to send him my resume when I got home so he could let me know of any jobs in the area that might be appropriate for me.

When I returned to Portland and told my relatives what I'd done, my cousin Moshe, who'd been active in the Oregon Democratic Party for decades, told me he had contacts "down there," and to let him know if he could do anything to help me get established; but his father, my then 91-year-old great-uncle Reuben, an attorney who had lived in Oregon all his adult life, told me to keep my head down. "It's not a place for Jews," he said. I had no idea what he meant by this and should have asked, but I would soon find out.

We left Vermont on July 4, 1990, and camped out along the way. Jim drove a big U-Haul truck full of our furniture and other belongings, and I drove my car, accompanied by the two children, our dog Molly, and our two cats Spike and Doodly-Doo. We had a good time traveling and arrived in pretty good shape. Once we had moved everything in, Jim flew back to St. Johnsbury, where we had put our house on the market. When he left Oregon, it was unclear what he would do if and when the house sold, but he had decided to retire from NEKCA and join us eventually.

I got us settled in Lincoln City and the kids started school, Daniel in first grade, Elizabeth in fifth. I got a good job as director of the Lincoln County Children and Youth Commission, and started work October 1 in Newport, about twenty-five miles to the south. I would quickly learn all the problems of Lincoln County, where the seasonal jobs in the tourist trade were generally low paying, and the problems that often go along with economic stress were rampant. Lincoln County, it turned out, had the highest per capita rate of drug and alcohol abuse, suicide, teen suicide, teenage parents, divorce, single-parent families, and adolescent AIDS in the state.[23]

About six months after our arrival I got a call from Smokey Aschenbrenner, whom I had run into on a fairly regular basis since our move and with whom I had struck up a casual friendship. He said there was a vacancy on the Lincoln City City Council due to the resignation of one of the councilors from Ward III, which comprised the southern end of Lincoln City. He and a few others wanted to talk to me about running for the seat, which would be decided in a special election in May.

Having moved to Lincoln City from St. Johnsbury, where you'd be laughed out of town if you so much as thought about running for a position on the selectboard after you'd lived in town for barely six months, I thought it was an insane idea but politely agreed to hear them out.

When we met, they made their pitch: Lincoln City was a town of transients and visitors, and nobody much would care how long I had lived there because so many of them were newcomers and part-time residents themselves. Furthermore, there was an urgent need for a community and family-minded candidate, because the council was heavily stacked at the

---

[23] Gary O. Larson, "Lifelong Journey: An Education in the Arts," National Endowment for the Arts, ED 425 991, SO 028 468 (1994).

moment with members who were pro-development at any cost, and who were willing to sacrifice the livability of the city and the beauty of its environment for increased profits. They promised to support me, and if I ran a good campaign, they thought there was a chance I could win.

My opponent, who had already announced her candidacy, would be Phyllis "P. J." Chessman, whose family had founded the nearby town of Gleneden Beach. She was a ten-year resident of Lincoln City, a former Chamber of Commerce "Woman of the Year," current chair of the city's Visitor and Convention Committee, and a member of the Bay Area Merchant Association, the Urban Renewal Advisory Committee, the North Lincoln Hospital Auxiliary, and the boards of directors for the North Lincoln County Museum and the Oregon Coast Council for the Arts. I thought it would be a losing battle, but I've never been one to avoid a challenge, and Smokey and his friends were insistent.

They had of course not sought me out entirely out of the blue. As he had requested, I'd sent Smokey my resume, and it would have been obvious to him from reading it that politics was in my blood. Furthermore, in my short time in Lincoln County I had already gained some attention as a champion of the needs of working families from my well-publicized appointment as director of the Children and Youth Commission, and from a project I had initiated in my neighborhood, organizing new friends and neighbors to petition the city to let us create a community park and playground on a vacant double lot that the city owned.

My platform, not surprisingly, was to provide representation for families and other long-term residents of Lincoln City to assure that their needs were not overlooked in the city council's conversation about how to attract and provide for more tourists. That meant working toward a more diverse economy and for aggressive recruitment of businesses and clean industry that would create stable, year-round employment. I also questioned the pending relocation of city hall and the city library away from the southern end of town, which seemed like it would hasten the slump already starting to occur in our area.

I knocked on every door in Cutler City, Taft, and Nelscott, the three southernmost and least populated areas of the city, which made up Ward III. I introduced myself and explained why Ward III needed representation that would provide a counterbalance to the current emphasis on tourism. As far as I could tell, my opponent did nothing. I'm sure she found the notion of my winning the election beyond anything she could imagine. Nonetheless, when the votes were counted on May 21, I had beaten her 225 to 173. I would win reelection to a full term in January 1993.

At first all went well. I enjoyed the city council and felt I was making a contribution to our usually thoughtful debate about the many economic challenges facing the city and the pros and cons of each proposal for meeting them. The Cutler City park and playground idea had received city backing, and an enthusiastic group of over forty men, women, and children—backed up by city excavating crews—had created an attractively fenced in playground, basketball court, and picnic area, which was named "Kids Park and Seniors Too," the winning name having been submitted by an eight-year-old boy who won a $50 gift certificate for his idea.

The park was dedicated on March 21, 1992, and the neighborhood group, pleased with its new sense of community, continued meeting to talk about other local issues, ranging from zoning controversies and unwanted development to parenting issues and healthy social opportunities for our children. We formed a "Kids Council" and began to use the Community Club—a small building in the center of the neighborhood—for meetings and occasional events.

The Community Club had an interesting history. It had originally been one of the small cottages, but had been deeded to the residents of Cutler City by its owner, to be used as a social hall. It had fallen into disuse for its intended purpose some years before and came into the hands of people not necessarily from the neighborhood, who had joined the club, taken over as its officers, and started running a bingo game there three nights a week. We had no intention of interfering with the bingo games, but we did want to use the clubhouse when it was otherwise available, and felt this was an activity squarely within the purpose for which the club had been donated, as spelled out in its deed and charter.

However, when we approached the bingo people hoping to come up with a regular meeting schedule for the Kids Council, they quickly made it clear that they had no intention of graciously sharing the building. They seemed very nervous about how strong a sense of community the neighborhood was developing, and were very unpleasant to all of us who were part of the new group.

One night the bingo people showed up at a party the kids had organized and were very inappropriate in their language and behavior. A week later the officers showed up at one of our regular meetings with a large group of bingo players, intent on taking over our meeting. When they realized that we weren't an official club with a membership they could infiltrate, their first two disruptions were followed by threatening phone calls to those of us who shared leadership of the group. The callers would tell us to "lay off bingo," and then hang up. This left us a little perplexed, since we felt there was plenty of time in the week for both groups to meet their needs for space.

As our group held meetings and negotiating sessions with the officers of the club, it soon became clear that I was the primary target of the bingo people, and was being blamed for everything. An artist who lived in the neighborhood and had been one of the co-leaders of our group from the beginning, had been recruiting people from the neighborhood to infiltrate the bingo club and give them a dose of their own medicine. However, in our negotiating sessions, it was I who was blamed for this attempt to "take over the club," even though my artist friend readily admitted that it had been her idea and her doing, and that I had tried to dissuade her from this effort. I was also accused of trying to "shut down bingo," even though I had been outspoken in my belief that bingo was a good activity to have available for the seniors who lived in the neighborhood.

Then, in what seemed like a very strange twist, one of the bingo women was said to have accused me, in my capacity as a city councilor, of taking away the city employees' Christmas bonuses. When I confronted her she said that "someone in administration" had told her that. She was also quoted as having said at a meeting of the club that "someone downtown says she's trouble," referring to me. Because her husband was the chair of the planning commission, and I had recently been successful in having the city council appoint an environmental protection task force to identify those areas of the city that needed to be protected from development, I began to understand that there was a lot more going on than a simple disagreement over who should be able to use the clubhouse when.

Then word reached me that this same woman was said to have referred to me as "that woman from New York"—a code phrase my older and more streetwise husband informed me had long been used as an anti-Semitic slur. How did these people even know I was Jewish? Of course! Since our arrival, I'd been bothered by the fact that much of Oregon was increasingly being dominated by the religious right. We saw it in the schools, and we saw it in local government. I had felt moved to organize the first-ever community *seder* on the central Oregon coast, putting a notice in the paper with my name as the contact person. It was a huge success, with nearly one hundred people in attendance. Clearly, the bingo people's resistance to our use of the clubhouse was becoming more and more complex and the stakes higher and higher.

Then, on August 10, I received a call at work from a Lincoln City police officer, who said he was calling from my house in Lincoln City, where Daniel was at home with a babysitter. The officer wanted my permission to have Daniel open our mailbox, so he could perhaps seize a letter. The other city councilor from our ward, a longtime Cutler City resident, had received a threatening letter that morning in a very distinctive envelope, having to do with the Community Club controversy. He had identified me to the police as someone else who might have received a similar one. Of course I agreed, and the officer soon returned to the phone to say that indeed there was such a letter, and he wanted to take it for fingerprinting. Again I agreed.

When I got home I quickly learned that two others had received similar letters, for a total of four. Arriving in envelopes addressed in red block letters executed with the apparent aid of a stencil, and with an upside down (dead?) duck stamp on each one, my fellow councilor's letter said, "TURNCOAT S.O.B. YOUR TIME IS REAL SOON BACK OFF." The artist's letter said "BUSYBODY CUNT. YOUR ART DAYS ARE FEW—BACK OFF BINGO BITCH! LIKE NO FINGERS." Our neighbors' letter said, "DO GOODER ASSHOLES! WE WARNED YOU! YOU'RE NO. 1." I figured the content of my own letter wouldn't be good either.

The following day, before I left for work, I called the police department and asked if my letter had been opened. Yes, I was told, it had been opened and fingerprinted, but they couldn't tell me the content. So I was totally unprepared when I ran into my neighbor that evening heading for a meeting of our group. Carrying a fistful of papers, she told me how awful she felt about my letter. I said I hadn't seen my letter and didn't know what it said. She then handed me a copy, explaining that she had been up at the police station that afternoon and had been given copies of all of them. My letter read: "JEW BITCH! NO MORE WARNINGS YOU'RE NO. 2."

It's not possible to adequately describe in writing what happened next. Upon reading my letter, I was suddenly overwhelmed by a powerful emotion that I couldn't remember ever having felt before, and couldn't identify. I could feel it pushing me rapidly into a physical panic response, as I was finding it difficult to breathe and could feel my heart racing. Feelings I never knew I had about being Jewish were suddenly in my face, and I couldn't even guess where they were coming from.

Because of the religious reference and the use of the U.S. mail to send the letter, my neighbor told me, mine was a felony hate crime, whereas the other three only constituted harassment, a misdemeanor. She added that the police chief, upon hearing the entire story of the bingo war, had also added a count of "intimidating a public official" in my case and the other councilor's, and was "boiling mad," she said, as he, too, was committed to keeping Lincoln City a livable place for the permanent residents.

I mumbled something in my neighbor's general direction about having forgotten my pen, ran back inside my house, called the police station, and left a very irritated message for the chief saying that I didn't understand why I'd been denied a copy of my letter when my neighbors were walking around with copies of their letters *and* mine, and why was my personal mail being distributed to other people anyway? I felt totally out of control and could tell that my neck and face were red as a beet.

When I had calmed down some I walked over to the meeting, where most of the group had already assembled. But as I walked into the living room that same emotion overwhelmed me again and I found I couldn't look at any of them. I felt that everyone who looked at me was thinking "there goes the Jew." I walked straight through to the kitchen and helped myself to a glass of water. As I drank it, looking out the window, I overheard someone in the living room say, "she's embarrassed," and I remember thinking it odd at the time—why would I be embarrassed? I considered myself a secular Jew with a relationship to Judaism that pretty much began and ended with the celebration of Chanukah and Passover in my home. Why was I now being defined by the fact that I was Jewish? It didn't make sense to me.

In fact, as I would later learn when I sought professional help for recurrences of this emotional reaction, shame and guilt are classic responses of post-traumatic stress disorder, and self-blame for one's victimization a particularly common aspect of PTSD when the victimization is based on a personal characteristic that is unchangeable or out of one's control, such as race or religion.

The truth is, the hateful letter I received back then had a profound and enduring effect on me, although at the time I had no idea this would be so. All I knew then was that these physical symptoms were overwhelming me because I was Jewish, and as that thought sank in as I sat there in the living room, I silently became more and more distraught.

Talk that evening focused on what the police chief had said to the others that afternoon: Take all possible precautions, and consider further danger very possible. In addition to their tax exemption having been taken away for lack of any charitable work, it seemed that the bingo games were taking in a lot more money than they were declaring. The police had them under investigation for that reason. I took it all in, but was unable to say much.

The following day the four of us who had received letters met with the police chief, and in addition to repeating his earlier warnings, he suggested we all carry mace as a precaution, just in case. He told us that because the mailing of my letter was a felony hate crime, and because two of us were public officials, the FBI had agreed to get involved and would be contacting us. Perhaps meant to soothe us, this new information raised the level of anxiety we were all feeling.

I went home and called the nearby Jewish camp where Elizabeth was a camper. I needed to talk to someone else who was Jewish, and I needed to know that Elizabeth was safe. I was glad I had called when the director said that they would go into lockdown, just in case. As he explained, their experience was that such action by one crazy person encourages actions by others, and the camp was a big target. Meanwhile, Daniel was reluctant to let me out of his sight, and was begging me not to walk the dog around the block at night without first taking precautions.

I'm happy to say that two days after the letters were received the Lincoln City weekly, the *News Guard*, ran a very supportive editorial entitled "A Cowardly Act," coming down hard on the perpetrators and insisting that Lincoln City was better than this. Following the editorial there were no further threatening calls or letters for the next ten days, and things seemed to quiet down. Then, just as we were beginning to feel normal again and enjoying a potluck dinner in the neighborhood, fire engines raced into Cutler City. Running after them, we found our neighbor's house on fire. The fire was ruled suspicious, but nothing could be proved one way or another.

A week later the bingo people decided to move their game to the north end of Lincoln City, and no further incidents occurred. We all gradually went back to our normal lives and tried to forget the whole thing. Neither the police investigation nor the FBI inquiry ever came up with anything solid, but I was left subject to flare-ups of my victimization response, often to the surprise of family, friends, and colleagues, who were at a loss to understand my occasionally disproportionate reactions to things that didn't seem to warrant them.

*   *   *

It was about this time that I read in the *News Guard* that volunteers were needed for an archaeological excavation not far down the coast near Yachats at Cape Perpetua in the Siuslaw National Forest. I hadn't been on a dig since my first one in Israel, but badly needing a break from real life I signed up for a five-day stint sponsored by the U.S. Forest Service as part of its "Passport In Time" program. It was a relaxed and congenial group and just what I needed. Our supervisor was happy to let me return to Lincoln City on Friday night and bring Daniel back to share the experience for the last two days. He applied himself well and did me proud. In fact, it was such a successful joint adventure for us that I went online when I got home and found a second PIT project to work on over his spring break from school. This one was in the Tonto National Forest near Superior, Arizona, in the Superstition Mountains.

The work in Arizona was to have been stabilizing the Rogers Canyon cliff dwellings and recording the petroglyphs there, but when we arrived at the Forest Service office we were quickly informed that due to the unusual amount of rain they'd had for the past several weeks, the steep descent was too treacherous for the burros who were to carry in our heavy gear, and stabilizing the cliff dwellings was out of the question. If we wanted to hike in without the burros, packing in our personal gear and the lighter equipment on our backs to just do the petroglyph recording, we'd have to repack to eliminate what we could and agree to live as communally and frugally as possible. I sized Daniel up and decided there was no reason we couldn't continue. I knew he was a very focused and hard worker for his age and size, and wouldn't present any problems.

The next morning we set off single file with the others. The trail was challenging, primarily because even in the best of weather it crosses a stream twenty-six times and at this moment the stream was abnormally high, swollen, and raging. Daniel, with all the alacrity of an eight-year-old in his element, took to hopping across the stream from rock to rock and boulder to boulder, whether they were submerged or not, then turning around and hopping halfway back to a point where he could hold out his hand to help me along. This went on for over three hours, until we finally reached our destination and set up camp. The rest of the project was anticlimactic.

*   *   *

My Oregon work life, the first year, was a real pleasure. I enjoyed my job with the Children and Youth Commission, which allowed me to meet a lot of people and get to know this new area where I was living. It was interesting to see how working in a large and diverse state differed from working in Vermont, where everything felt like it was the work of a small community, with all the pluses and minuses that implied. I also liked being in an area with a significant Native American population and having the opportunity to begin to learn their customs, as well as understand their particular needs and concerns.

One custom I became very familiar with was the lighting of bundles of sage prior to the start of a meeting. This was explained to me as a way to clear the air of negative thoughts and feelings that might be present and likely to get in the way of productive work. After experiencing the sage ceremony several times I came to see it as very worthwhile, at a minimum halting all miscellaneous pre-meeting chatter and redirecting participants' thoughts to the matter at hand.

Another memorable lesson came from a Native American speaker at a meeting of the State Children and Youth Commission. When introduced at the start of the meeting he asked for understanding from the audience, explaining that it was difficult for him to participate in a meeting like this, where he was asked to sit on a stage above the audience as if he had both the authority to answer our questions and the right answers to give. He contrasted a typical meeting in what he referred to as the dominant culture, where competing individuals attempt to sway the decision making by stating their opinions with as much authority as possible, to the ways of Native Americans, who sit in a circle, hear from each participant in turn, and look back seven generations for guidance. That contrast of arrogance and modesty has stayed with me to this day, and I am often reminded of it at meetings that include participants with big egos who like to hear themselves speak.

As part of my job I met frequently with other social service administrators to develop an application for a demonstration grant from the federal Center for Alcohol and Drug Abuse Programs. We came up with a countywide project that would bring $400,000 in alcohol and drug abuse prevention services into the county annually for five years, if we were awarded the grant.

As the project took shape, I became very excited about its possibilities. It was designed to be a community-based collaboration of public and nonprofit service providers, city officials, and private individuals, guided by community organizers assigned to each of the four largest towns in the county, working under the direction of autonomous local alcohol and drug task forces in each area.

I got so excited in fact, that when the grant came through, I decided to apply for the job of director of the Lincoln County Partnership, as the new project was called. Since the Children and Youth Commission would be the grantee agency, this would make whoever replaced me as director of the commission my new boss to some extent, although supervision of me would be limited to the oversight of finances. It didn't seem a situation fraught with danger.

It did turn out to be an exciting, if difficult, project. I was deeply committed to the goal of it being not just community based but community run, by local groups truly representative of the four towns in which we would work. Selecting the steering committee that would oversee the project and put together those local groups was a delicate task, but the outcome was terrific, and I couldn't have asked for a better group of people to work with. I then turned my attention to hiring staff, and in the same spirit intentionally set out to hire as community organizers, four people as different from each other as I could find, but each with a deep and shared commitment to the goal and objectives of the Partnership. The great differences in age, experience, and lifestyle of the community organizers we selected made supervision a constant challenge, and at times I questioned my hiring wisdom, but it had the desired effect on our acceptance in the communities where we worked, and in our ability to pull into the project a very diverse group of people.

One interesting experience I had in the course of my work with the Partnership stemmed from a chance encounter with Alberta Tinsley-Williams. Tinsley-Williams, a Detroit activist I had grown to admire by reputation, addressed the 1992 Oregon State Prevention Conference dressed in sneakers and sweats. She had decided, she said, that "when you dress for war, you don't wear panty hose." Sitting in the audience wearing panty hose, and having spent most of my life at war with one thing or another despite having often been dressed in that way, I found her remarks offensive and more than a little naïve. The theme of the conference was "Building Bridges." Does it build bridges to write off all people in panty hose? I think not.

The Tinsley-Williams incident reminded me of an exchange that had occurred more than ten years earlier, and had a similar theme, but made me feel supported and understood in my personal choices. I had just started my clerkship at the Vermont Supreme Court and knew that the experience and contacts to be gained from clerking for the chief justice could only help me be more effective in my future work, whatever it might be.

However, not everyone had understood it that way. Some had suggested I was selling out the powerless and disenfranchised people I had worked so hard for in the past, in favor of a likely more lucrative career among the legal elite. So I felt somewhat defensive when one day I ran into the deputy director of Vermont Legal Aid on a stairway landing in the Supreme Court building. I was dressed formally for my courtroom rotation, and after exchanging greetings he asked me curiously what I was doing there. When I told him I had a clerkship with the Chief that year he didn't miss a beat, replying with a grin, "bore from within, bore from within." He himself went on to become a member of the Vermont judiciary, ending his career as a presiding judge.

There are those who wage war from the outside, there are those who bore from within, and there are those who can do both and still be believable, even if they sometimes wear panty hose. That, really, is what broad-based organizing is about. It's about recognizing that everyone has different skills, abilities, beliefs, and experiences that they bring to a task or problem, and that the more ways these can be utilized, the faster you all will reach your desired end.

The Partnership position might have worked out for me for the entire five years of the project, but for a poor initial hiring decision by the Children and Youth Commission. The person hired to replace me as its director had been a candidate for the job at the time I was hired and had been found not to be qualified. One year later she was still not qualified, but this time around the pool of applicants was smaller, and in addition she was rumored to be in a relationship with the county commissioner who had taken over administrative responsibility for the program.

I did not know all this at the time, but when I learned of it, it explained a lot of what subsequently occurred. She insisted on taking over more and more control of the Partnership, with the commissioner's support, but was not in tune with its philosophical grounding in the communities it served. We constantly butted heads as I fought to preserve the decision-making authority of the local committees. The Partnership steering committee was wonderfully supportive, but in the end their status as community volunteers was just not enough to put a stop to what was happening with official approval. I resigned in May 1993 after a year and a half on the job.

Jim and I weighed the relative merits of staying in Lincoln City and finding something else for me to do, moving to a new community, or returning to Vermont. Jim and the kids were all for returning to Vermont, but I was reluctant. There had been an important reason why we moved west, and the significantly stepped up family contact had been wonderful. But what would I find to do if we stayed? The county administered most of the programs I'd be interested in, but working for the county clearly wasn't going to be a realistic option in the near future. Moving to yet another new community felt like an exhausting undertaking, not to mention the strain it would put on our finances. Finally, I gave in to the others and agreed to move back to Vermont.

I still consider the move we made to Oregon to have been a good decision. There were many things about our three years there that we not only enjoyed, but thrived on. Being a stone's throw from the ocean was a wonderful experience. Jim made good and lasting friends at his part-time job at the library. We traveled a great deal when we could, and more than met the goal of connecting the kids with my family. Strong relationships were formed at an age when they would be remembered.

One of the most exciting things for all of us, and certainly for both kids, was the Oregon coast's large population of artists of all kinds. We were especially connected to the Oregon Coast Council for the Arts (OCCA) in nearby Newport. Elizabeth had always exhibited a flair for the dramatic, and at the suggestion of OCCA's Executive Director Sharon Morgan, who I came to know through my work with the Children and Youth Commission, she auditioned for a holiday production of *The Snow Queen*, and as the Little Robber Girl, brought down the house at the Newport Performing Arts Center. After that she was cast as the young daughter of a funeral home director in a TV pilot, "Whitewater," which launched her on a path that took her through many performances with the St. Johnsbury Players and ACT REAL when we returned to Vermont, and later with the University of Wisconsin's theatre department.

Daniel's artistic endeavors took a different form: the circus arts. OCCA had received funding from the U.S. Department of Agriculture to establish a summer program in the circus arts, primarily, but not exclusively, for at-risk kids. For an energetic boy with a father the age of most of his classmates' grandfathers, it was ideal. He excelled in the program. He learned juggling and clowning, but best of all he learned to ride a unicycle. Soon he was unicycling around Cutler City to the delight of the neighborhood, and he, too, brought his new skills back to Vermont when we returned.

Our home in Goss Hollow

Chapter Eleven

Some People Just Don't Get It

1993-1999

We returned to Vermont and settled into an old Victorian house on Cliff Street in the heart of St. Johnsbury in the late summer of 1993. I liked living in town and the sense of community it gave me to be able to walk everywhere and greet people as I went, but our long-term goal was to buy back the house we had built in Goss Hollow, which was for sale when we returned, but at a price we couldn't afford. I had designed the house, and friends from Mad Brook Farm had built it for us in 1980. We hoped if we waited it out the owners would lower the price and eventually that's what happened. We were back in Goss Hollow four years after we left.

Meanwhile, I needed to stretch my legs and find something creative to do. A cabin that was rotting away in the middle of the woods at Mad Brook Farm caught my interest, and I got permission from its owner to see what I could do with it. It was saturated with water and some of its interior walls could be pulled apart by hand; the center section of the roof boards had caved in, and the stairs to the door some five feet up in the air were falling off the front, among other things. But most of the infrastructure, consisting of hand-hewn 8"x8" posts and beams, and many of the exterior walls, were still sound, if unfinished. I figured there wasn't anything I could do to it that would make it worse, adjusted the design to something I thought I could execute, and have continued to work on it for over twenty-five years, a day here and a day there, becoming its official owner in 2010. Even without electricity or water it's now quite a respectable cabin.

I wanted to return to the practice of law but with more adequate support than I'd had in my previous attempt to be a sole practitioner. Bob Gensburg, one of the partners I'd started my legal career with, was now on his own and offered me an office plus the support of his staff so I could get going again. I remained there until Bob took on an associate and my work went in a direction that made a home office feasible, then set up my work space in our house, where it remained until I retired.

It felt good to be my own boss again and to be able to decide what kind of work I wanted to do. In 1996 I accepted a position with Vermont Assistance Inc. (VAI), an interdenominational faith-based nonprofit, whose sole purpose was to raise enough money each year to hire a lobbyist to work on legislative issues on behalf of low-income Vermonters. The position was part time, with most of the work occurring in the winter when the legislature was in session. VAI was my employer, and its members served as a resource for me, but the setting of legislative priorities and all substantive decision making was left to VLIAC (Vermont Low Income Advocacy Council), the same organization of low-income representatives from local chapters around the state that I had been a member of twenty-five years earlier, representing the Northeast Kingdom.

The VAI board was an exceptional group of people. Led by the Rev. John Nutting, during my time the board included three other ministers, a rabbi, several lay church leaders, the outspoken president of VLIAC, Edna Fairbanks Williams, and several people very savvy about the ways of Vermont state government, including David Wilson, my old friend from the McCarthy campaign, who was now Governor Howard Dean's secretary of administration. I met with VAI monthly, but took my day-to-day direction during the legislative session from VLIAC.

It was good to be back in the political arena and advocating for low-income Vermonters. In my new role I served as a resource for VLIAC as it developed its legislative priorities each fall, and during my tenure we held "A Day for Economic Justice" at the beginning of each legislative session. Low-income Vermonters descended on Montpelier from all directions for brief and intense workshops on key issues and lobbying techniques, then flooded the Statehouse to present their needs to their representatives.

Mostly, my job required camping out in the House and Senate Appropriations Committees for four to six months each year to monitor budgetary changes in everything from welfare benefits to funding for affordable housing, and staying in close contact with VLIAC in order to respond quickly to proposed changes in pending legislation. Forced to overcome my lifelong fear of math, I learned to read the state budget, studied it in minute detail, and came to know where and how money could be manipulated to fund our requests.

More than the citizen legislators, Governor Howard Dean was a major problem where support for low-income Vermonters was concerned. Many progressives had supported Dean when he ran for governor, and would do so again when he ran for president in 2004, and indeed he had a good record of supporting prevention-based programs and services for children and families, as these were based on a medical model he understood as a physician.

But Dean was hopelessly limited by his own experience: that of an affluent physician who had attended boarding school and an Ivy

League college, and who seemed ignorant of the roots and dynamics of multigenerational poverty, of which Vermont had, and still has, a great deal. As VLIAC's lobbyist I went after the governor and his budget mercilessly in our *ACTION ALERT* newsletter, realizing that I was likely dashing any slight chance I might still have had of becoming a Vermont judge someday, but keenly aware of my obligation to my clients and propelled by my personal belief in the legitimacy of their demands.

I learned the ropes in the House Appropriations Committee as I sought to monitor the committee's fast-paced decision making and interject pertinent information into its discussions at just the right moment. Nearly all the committee members were willing to help at key points, with even the most conservative member an ally in our effort to expand grant funding for the Vermont Student Assistance Corporation, to put higher education, and therefore eventual self-sufficiency, within reach of low-income students. In the Senate Appropriations Committee I found the chairman to be the most helpful once he fully understood the backstory to our issues.

It first shocked, then continued to amaze me, how little knowledge the average legislator has about what he or she is asked to vote on. But as I got to know many legislators personally, I came to understand it. Vermont's legislators are, for the most part, ordinary people. They come to the task of having to vote on hundreds of bills covering everything from child care subsidies to the length of the deer hunting season to the need for a new bridge in some far-off corner of the state, with no more knowledge about the pros and cons of the issues than the average person on the street. They have been elected for their openness, and for their good judgment, which their constituents hope they will exercise carefully and cautiously, and most do. I rarely met a legislator who wasn't willing to listen to an explanation of why some change under consideration was needed or not. And if that explanation was provided by a constituent who would be directly affected, no matter how plain spoken and unpolished that person might be, so much the better.

During the first year I lobbied for VLIAC the biggest issue we took on was getting an increase in ANFC, Vermont's welfare program. The governor's budget that year included inflationary increases for just about everything *but* ANFC families, whose benefits he proposed to level fund on the heels of a 3 percent cut the previous year. At the time the Department of Social Welfare was documenting that one in every six Vermonters was in need of public assistance of some kind, up from one in seven the year before, so Dean's lack of interest in sharing Vermont's wealth with its most needy citizens drew fire in VLIAC's newsletter:

> Since Gov. Dean is smart enough to know that the cost of food, clothing, and shelter increases for poor families along with everyone else, we can only conclude that he just doesn't care that tens of thousands of Vermonters are slipping further into poverty with his complicity…What makes the Gov's refusal to share the State's good times with poor families even more shameful, is that the money is there to pay for it. General Fund revenues are expected to top earlier projections this year by $6.5 million. The net effect, given the Gov's tight budget, is to bloat his Rainy Day Fund to $21.2 million this year, with more to come next year, and no rainy day in sight.[24]

---

[24] VLIAC *ACTION ALERT,* No. 3, February 12, 1997, 1-2.

When the senate initially failed to support even a 2 percent restoration, saying there must be a more creative and lasting solution to poverty, the decision to side with Dean in the face of an admitted awareness of the consequences of level funding made us angry and we said so:

> Poverty is, after all, about money. The more money you have, the less impoverished you are. And we think it's unlikely that the Vermont Senate is going to come up with an answer to the root causes of poverty in the next few weeks. Meanwhile, our low-income families are faced with the nearly impossible task of meeting their essential needs with dwindling resources. [25]

It was sad to see Vermont, led by Governor Dean, enter the race to the bottom with such aplomb.

The following year VLIAC trained its sights on increasing the General Assistance (GA) personal needs allowance. GA is a program that supports adults without children who cannot work because of incapacity or an emergency expected to last at least thirty days. A large number of GA recipients are individuals who have become permanently disabled and have applied for SSI or Social Security disability benefits, but whose applications have not yet been approved. Others might have experienced a catastrophic event such as a fire that has destroyed their home and possessions. Nonetheless, because these recipients are adults who aren't gainfully employed when they apply and have no children to feed, they are wrongly assumed by many to be undeserving.

---

[25] VLIAC *ACTION ALERT*, No. 6, April 21, 1997, 2.

The GA personal needs allowance, which has to cover everything a person might need except food and rent, was just $10.50/week and had not been increased for twenty-four years! Once brought to their attention, our friends on the House Appropriations Committee quickly realized the absurdity of anyone trying to live on this amount of money, and voted to increase the monthly allowance to $70. Not so the senate, which saw affirmative votes by only two members of its Appropriations Committee. It took the firmness of the House Appropriations chair and her colleagues to get a conference committee compromise of $56/month. Little enough!

After three years of lobbying for VLIAC while trying to maintain my private law practice, I decided not to renew my contract. The work was easily taking up half the year starting in late fall with presession meetings of the House Appropriations Committee and meetings with VLIAC to set priorities, and then running well into mid-May with follow-up newsletters. Jim was approaching seventy now, and since our return to Vermont had been working only half time at a low-paying job and had no retirement savings at all. I had my disability work and had also been appointed an appellate officer for the Vermont secretary of state's office to hear appeals from decisions of Vermont's professional licensing boards. But to say we were cobbling things together financially was an understatement, and with Elizabeth about to head to college and Daniel a few years behind her, I needed to generate more income for the family.

After taking a week to clear my head of legislative issues with another PIT project at Kentucky Camp in the Coronado National Forest, south of Tucson, I returned to St. Johnsbury and heard about a group of social service agency people, educators, and St. Johnsbury town officials who had been meeting to brainstorm ways to counteract a gang culture that had developed in the area as a result of drugs being transported from Canada to Boston and New York City via I-91.

The work of the group coincided with an initiative being undertaken by the Vermont Department of Corrections (DOC) to provide a better alternative to the existing system for processing juveniles who had committed delinquent acts. A pilot program in Burlington, called the Burlington Community Justice Center, had been organized around restorative justice principles and was showing good results. The St. Johnsbury group had just formed a board to develop its own community justice center, and with financial backing from DOC was looking for a part-time director. I applied and was hired to serve as the founding director.

I served as director of the CJC for a total of eight years. Like the other CJCs that eventually formed around the state, our mainstay programs were reparative boards for both juveniles and adults, and a reentry program that supported adult offenders returning to the community from jail. What made the St. Johnsbury CJC stand out, however, were its other initiatives: a free monthly legal clinic staffed by volunteer attorneys; free mediation services; development and support of neighborhood associations in four areas of the town; trainings provided for school personnel in restorative discipline; truancy conferences for local schools; and a Parking Board to which St. Johnsbury parking tickets could be appealed.

Sad to say, despite our best efforts, the principles of restorative justice never quite caught on among the community at large, and in this result—or lack of it—I believe our experience was similar to that of other CJCs elsewhere in the state. The people who serve on reparative boards or attend restorative conferences almost always emerge from the experience impressed with the meaningful communication that occurs between victims and offenders, and the creative ways in which offenders can make amends for their actions. But society as a whole clings stubbornly to punishment as the intervention of choice, and it seems that most cannot be convinced to let go.

Caledonia County Fair parade led by Daniel and Elizabeth

Chapter Twelve

Big Losses and Little Victories

2000-2002

I n 1999, the same year I started work at the Justice Center, the Vermont Supreme Court decided the case of *Baker v. State,* which held that same-sex couples must be granted the same benefits and protections that heterosexual couples enjoy under the state's marriage laws. The Court did not require the state to allow same-sex marriage, but directed the legislature to come up with an equivalent process by which same-sex couples would have the same legal status as if they were married.

Governor Dean made it clear that he would veto anything called "marriage." This led to passage the following year, 2000, of An Act Relating to Civil Unions, which gave town clerks the authority to issue licenses to same-sex couples for civil unions, in the same way they would issue marriage licenses to heterosexual couples. Same-sex couples could then be legally joined by anyone authorized to perform marriages under state law, and such unions could only be terminated by divorce in the same way that heterosexual couples could terminate their marriages. Passage made Vermont the first state to recognize the right of same-sex couples to enter into marriage-like unions.

It was nowhere near as simple an achievement as it sounds now. Once the Court's decision came down, opponents of same-sex marriage went to work to prevent the proposed legislation from seeing the light of day. In this they had the help of national right-wing groups determined not to let any state succeed in such an endeavor. These groups poured money into the state and denounced gays and lesbians as abominations, saying that allowing civil unions would send the state down an immoral path of no return. Some legislators who sponsored hearings on the bill in their districts said they feared physical harm, and Governor Dean took to wearing a bullet-proof vest.[26]

By the time final hearings were held by the legislature prior to the crucial votes in the house and senate, the national press had swarmed into Vermont and into the house chamber in particular, where the final hearing was held before hundreds of emotionally charged supporters and opponents. State police were planning for the possibility that the crowd would turn on one group of legislators or the other and had set up an escape route out of the building that legislators were told to take immediately if ordered to leave, no questions asked.[27]

I helped organize support for the bill in Caledonia County. Not only did I believe that one's sexual orientation had nothing to do with whether they should be able to enter into a relationship like marriage, but many of my Vermont friends as well as friends and relatives elsewhere were gay or lesbian, and it incensed me that anyone could be saying such horrible things about them. I passed petitions, wrote a letter to the editor, and kept a long list of people advised of upcoming hearings in Montpelier and the Northeast Kingdom they could attend. I felt a personal necessity to speak up at these hearings for those who were not publicly "out," or who did not feel they could speak for themselves in public.

---

[26] Liz Halloran, "How Vermont's 'Civil War' Fueled the Gay Marriage Movement," National Public Radio, March 23, 2013.
[27] Ibid.

With great trepidation I set off for the Statehouse on March 15 with Elizabeth, who was home from college, for the final hearing and vote in the house. Standing squished together in the short corridor between the Card Room and the house chamber, I tried to calm her as she got angrier and angrier at legislator after legislator, occasionally ones she knew, who denounced the bill and said they would vote against it. To our shame, both of our local representatives, people we otherwise knew to be reasonable, voted against the bill, along with a longtime faculty member at St. Johnsbury Academy who had been dean of students during Elizabeth's time there. When others spoke passionately in favor of the legislation, and of course when the bill ultimately passed, tears of joy and relief ran down both our cheeks as we hugged each other and others nearby.

The public reaction to passage, and to Governor Dean's signing of the bill, continued to be strong and divided. The anti-civil union forces organized a movement that distributed TAKE BACK VERMONT signs that were then affixed to homes, barns, and front lawns throughout the state. A few can still be seen over twenty years later. As punishment for those Republicans who had voted in favor of the bill, a large amount of conservative money was poured into the fall election and succeeded in defeating all but one of the fourteen Republican house members who had done so, as well as some less entrenched Democratic legislators.

Although I could fairly be called a political veteran by the year 2000, I was shocked at the strength of the anti-civil union forces and the hatefulness of what I had seen during the legislative battle, and was determined to take whatever action I could to support and protect Vermont's new civil right. Once again, I decided that meant a run for the legislature, the only question being whether to run for the house or the senate. Both were two-seat districts; in the house I would be running against an incumbent Republican who had opposed the civil union bill, and a political newcomer, a moderate Republican whom I knew and liked but whom I suspected would not be one to stick his neck out any further than his predecessor had. In the senate I would be running against two Republican incumbents, both of whom had also voted against the bill.

This time I consulted with Paul Cillo, a ten-year Vermont legislator, house majority leader, and Northeast Kingdom resident who knew the people and the districts well. Paul's assessment was that if I ran for the house there was a chance I might win, but if I ran for the senate I would surely lose. But, he added, if I ran for the senate there was no doubt I would contribute a great deal to organizing a part of the state that had largely been ignored by the Democratic Party, a service that would pay off for years into the future.

It was a difficult decision. I wanted to win and was confident that I would be a good representative for either district, if only they would let me. I knew how conservative St. Johnsbury was, and thought my chances in other parts of the district might actually be better. I hoped Paul was wrong and that I could both win and make a larger contribution running for the senate, and I knew that as a senate candidate I could at least use my candidacy as a vehicle by which many more people could respond to the TAKE BACK VERMONT movement and make their positions known in November.

I announced my candidacy in the *Caledonian-Record* on May 24, 2000, and then leapt into action. Running for the senate was no small undertaking. The district comprised twenty-one towns in Caledonia and Orange counties, a couple of which I'd barely ever set foot in, and knew little or nothing about except that they were very small, very rural, and very conservative. Each town would require its own campaign committee to set up local speaking opportunities, advise me of local events where I could appear, and canvass door to door on my behalf. In addition, I needed to pull together quickly an overall campaign committee to help with message, strategy, literature and lawn sign design and distribution, media exposure, and press releases. It was a daunting prospect and would require a lot of committed people, but I was angry, inspired by the challenge, and ready to take it on.

I got on the phone and started making calls. The treasurer from my house campaign in 1988 and the person who had coordinated newspaper and radio ads for me in that race both agreed to take on those jobs again. The publisher of *New England Farmer* pulled together a handful of people knowledgeable in layout and wordsmithing, and together in a rough and tumble meeting at his house we came up with a handout that would be the cornerstone of our door-to-door campaign. The lieutenant governor, the Senate Appropriations Committee chair, and Vermont's commissioner of public service all provided quotes attesting to my ability to "get things done" in state government. And finally, if somewhat reluctantly, my dear friend and longtime fellow rabble-rouser, Sheila Reed, agreed to be my campaign manager, a post she very ably filled until she could no longer stand the bottomless "to do" lists I foisted on her, unfairly expecting her to become as relentlessly driven as I was, and politely bowed out.

For obvious reasons the gay and lesbian community and their allies were among the first to step up to help, holding house parties where their friends and acquaintances could meet me and we hoped be persuaded that I was a candidate worth actively backing. They were quickly followed by many of the women who had cut their political teeth on the Caledonia County Equal Rights Amendment campaign, many of whom were still involved in the Caledonia County Women's Network. People of all sizes, shapes, and ages came out of the woodwork to do whatever they did best on my behalf, and it was beyond gratifying. I can never thank all of those people adequately, but I hope they know who they are.

And we needed a lot of people. There were doors to knock on, lawn signs to distribute, personal letters to write to undecided voters, letters to the editor to submit, parades to march in, requests for absentee ballots to follow up on, get-out-the-vote phone calls to make, and on and on and on. Jim

Hughes from Fairlee ran as a Democrat for the second seat in the district, and ran a vigorous and coordinated campaign that helped considerably in the part of the district that was in Orange County; a friend wrote a wonderful feature article about me for the *North Star* weekly, which introduced me to its wide readership. Paul Cillo took on the job of organizing the town of Hardwick, which I knew meant that all I needed to do to win there was show up when and where he told me to and lay out my positions for those who came to listen. Democratic house candidates in my senate district invited me to campaign with them, and introduced me to their friends and neighbors; Bernie Sanders, then running for reelection to the U.S. House of Representatives, invited me to appear with him on several occasions, where he endorsed me.

One of the things I was most pleased with was the participation of my children, then 19 and 16, in my campaign. Elizabeth took a semester off from her studies at UW to help, and made it her particular business to register young people to vote and to make sure they voted for me. Going through St Johnsbury Academy yearbooks from years past, she made extensive use of the internet and reached out to people she knew, explaining to them why I should be their candidate, how to register to vote, and how to request an absentee ballot. Once they were successfully in my camp, she would then ask them for the names of more young people whom she could also contact. Since the Academy draws its students from many surrounding towns, her work undoubtedly accounted for a significant number of votes throughout the county.

Elizabeth also organized a young people's event for me, "Bread and Votes," at Northern Lights Bookstore and Cafe. Word got out and a crowd of enthusiastic young people gathered one evening for what was likely the first political event any of them had ever attended. I spoke about the issues that were not only near and dear to me but also ones that affected them, and

What a politician won't do for a vote! (top left) Wells River/Woodsville 4th of July celebration; (top right) Newark Street Fair Dunk Tank; (bottom) Caledonia County Fair Milking Contest

then we all listened to a band of musicians that had been pulled together for the occasion, while Elizabeth saw to registering new voters.

Daniel, who was a junior in high school at the time, was my most committed parade companion and could be counted upon to join a march or hold up his end of a banner whenever I needed him. He also recruited his friends at the Academy to help pull off a stunning display of lawn signs one morning. With prior approval from landowners, and thanks to the breadth of his and Elizabeth's contacts, area high school and college kids fanned out in all directions late one night to plant hundreds of my signs on lawns throughout the district—signs that hadn't yet made an appearance anywhere. Much to the amazement of commuting motorists driving to work the next morning the signs seemed to be everywhere! Feedback was that people were impressed with the apparent breadth, depth, and enthusiasm of my support.

I was able to find fun in the campaign as well. Why else would I have ever learned to milk a cow, if not to compete in the candidates' milking contest at the Caledonia County Fair? Not only had I never milked a cow before, I wasn't sure I had ever even been up close enough to one to touch it. I turned to my neighbors for help so that I wouldn't embarrass myself too badly, and they came through, teaching me to milk in their big barn at the bend in our road.

Then there was the Caledonia County Democrats' rally at the Burklyn Mansion on July 3, the Fourth of July parades in Woodsville/Wells River and later in the day in Groton, followed by a big chicken supper. I'll also never forget the Newark Street Fair's dunk tank that I braved with local house candidate Ken Gordon—no need to say any more about that! It was all in a day's work from July through November 7, 2000. When I look at photographs of friends and other people I don't even know, standing in the cold, late fall weather bundled up in coats and fur hats holding my signs in front of plant gates and at intersections, I can only hope that at least they had some fun, too.

So why didn't I win? According to Paul I never really had a chance: The incumbents were well known, it was just too conservative a district, and as yet totally unorganized by the Democrats in many areas. However, my decision to run for the senate rather than the house was somewhat vindicated; I lost in St. Johnsbury again by a substantial number of votes.

I received many cards and letters after the election attesting to the truth of Paul's assessment of my chances, as well as the validity of my decision, of which the following is a sample:

> It's difficult to maintain faith in humankind in the face of northeastern Vermont's voting… Alas, it brought out the worst in people. However, the campaign you ran and the issues you embodied made us enormously proud to have been your supporters. (Newbury voters).

> We wish to thank you for your efforts at representing us in Caledonia County. You made a lot of us quite excited at the prospect of having a bright and caring person on the front line…. No doubt your run for the Senate would have been successful in almost any other county in Vermont. Change is slow, isn't it? (Barnet voters)

> What a superb run for Vermont State Senate. Who would have thought a Democrat could pull so many votes from that staid area of the Northeast Kingdom. You helped prove that change is truly happening in this area and showed the entrenched they are out of step with what is going on. We believe your campaign has given hope to those who want to participate in true

democracy but have been long suppressed... Your efforts "sowed the seeds" of enlightenment and have reopened the intellectual freedom of choice for future elections for many. (Voters from unknown town)

But running for political office is a funny thing. Even if you don't expect to win when you start out, after months of being told what a wonderful person you are and what a great campaign you're running, you begin to think that maybe, just *maybe,* you can win, and I'd be lying if I said that I wasn't terribly disappointed on election night when I lost. Oh, I knew intellectually that it wasn't likely to happen, and I tried to prepare my kids especially, along with myself; but I hoped I might somehow be surprised, and I still think—all these years later—that I would have made an excellent state senator for my district.

The issues I have always cared most about are primarily low-wage working people's issues, and had the low-wage working people who lived in my district been able to stop chanting "TAKE BACK VERMONT" long enough to actually read and think about my positions on affordable health care and child care, minimum wage, family leave and other support for working families, or the need to support our local small business economy, I think they would have found much that they liked.

Fortunately, Paul's other prediction, that my campaign would go far to organize the district, also came true. No Democrat ran in 2002, but in 2004 Danville native Jane Kitchel was elected to the state senate, the first Democrat to be elected from Caledonia County in sixteen years. The district had been organized, and Kitchel inherited the results of that work; she went on to chair Vermont's Senate Appropriations Committee.

*   *   *

In early 2001 the Business and Professional Women's St. Johnsbury chapter did me the honor of nominating me for the Alice Paul Award, named for the woman who had fought so hard in the early 1900s for women's suffrage and equal rights, and who drafted the first federal Equal Rights Amendment in 1923. Letters supporting my nomination were sent in to the state organization from BPW members and nonmembers alike, extolling my virtues and enumerating my accomplishments in a way that had never been done before, according to the selection committee. I was overwhelmed when I read my copies of the letters they submitted, and found much food for thought in them.

K. C. Whiteley's letter spoke to the quality of fearlessness that she thought I possessed, and analyzed it this way:

> I believe this comes from her acceptance of and enthusiasm for differences, and a genuine compassion for others. She does not feel separate, or different, or better than other people, so she isn't afraid of, as many of us are, people who are unlike ourselves. This is one of the reasons why she is such an outstanding advocate and champion for equal rights for whomever the disadvantaged person or group is. She possesses an innate, intuitive sense that we are all connected and that one person's welfare is linked to and affects us all. You need only look at her diverse circle of friends to see how true this is.[28]

I have always felt Whiteley's analysis to be a particularly astute observation, and one which clarified for me why I have felt the way I have about some of the political figures I have supported over the years, most notably Gene McCarthy and Bernie Sanders. Both men saw each of us as

---

[28] K. C. Whiteley letter to Urie, February 26, 2001.

being connected, and one person's welfare as linked to everyone else's. Unfortunately, this was sometimes to their political detriment, because that philosophy, and their apparent lack of interest in seeking out and catering to special interest groups who might otherwise have helped them, was so poorly understood.

I did not receive the Alice Paul Award, but undaunted, the St. Johnsbury BPW chapter decided to nominate me for the state organization's Woman of the Year Award toward the end of the year. They synthesized the earlier letters of nomination into an amazingly coherent and flattering history of me, and added a few new letters of praise from friends who referred to me as the "preeminent social justice barometer," or said kind things about me like, "she does good works for no other agenda than making a difference."

Elizabeth, back in school in Madison, sent an email full of notes and anecdotes like the following:

> I remember my mother being very involved in every school I went to, always conscious of school policies which might disadvantage working mothers. I would come home from school and announce to my mom that there was an event at school some afternoon that week that she should come to, and she would ask me, "Well Elizabeth, how are the moms that have to work all day going to be able to come to that?" At eight years old I looked at her plaintively in response and didn't know what to say. Today, I still remember how concerned she was that every person, especially women, get equal opportunities and equal access.

It was of no lasting importance to me that the state BPW organization once again declined to honor me, but I would have liked it to happen for the sake of the local chapter and the women who twice supported me. In my low moments, when I think about lost opportunities and wonder why I didn't manage my life better, all I have to do is pull out these tangible pieces of evidence that my work has been appreciated by many to feel better about how I have lived my life and hope to be remembered.

*   *   *

Of course, as much as I was appreciated by my friends and many others in my community, my efforts were not appreciated by the conservative element in St. Johnsbury or by their mouthpiece, the *Caledonian-Record.* Among my friends and political associates, it was something of a badge of honor to be publicly criticized in "The Wrecker." It's never pleasant, however, to be attacked in print, knowing that the vast majority of readers will believe whatever they read in their local newspaper, right or wrong. I consoled myself over the years by thinking that the attacks must be a measure of my success; but that only helped a little, and the time came when I felt they'd crossed a line and I had to respond.

In 2002 I was serving as chair of the St. Johnsbury Town Democratic Committee when the time for party caucuses rolled around in late August. I realized that I would not be able to attend, as Daniel was starting college that fall in Oberlin, Ohio—a milestone event I was not about to miss—and we would be on the road delivering him there on the very date the caucuses were required to be held. I was not too concerned. The organization lay dormant most of the year and when there was real work to be done a group was rounded up to do it. So I left town having put the official notice of the caucus in the paper, made sure that all current members of the town committee were aware of it, and having indicated my interest in continuing to serve as one of St. Johnsbury's fifteen justices of the peace, who by "gentlemen's agreement" had for sixty years been equally allocated to the nominees of the Democratic and Republican town committees, with the fifteenth slot going to the party of the sitting governor.

Since I had worked tirelessly on behalf of Democratic candidates in virtually every local and statewide election since moving to town in 1980, except for the years we were gone, I felt this one absence was not a big deal and couldn't imagine it would jeopardize my nomination for the JP seat I had held for years and the place on the Board of Civil Authority that automatically went with it.

Wrong. I returned home to find that in my absence an ambitious friend who had said she'd make sure things went smoothly, had not only not supported my nomination for JP but had seen to her own nomination in my place. I was not happy. I felt that my rejection was unfair given all the work I had done on behalf of the committee and as a JP and member of the Board of Civil Authority, not to mention having put myself out there to run for office twice.

But the more I thought about it the more convinced I became that my putting myself out there was exactly the problem. As a JP I had been performing a lot of civil unions since the new law went into effect, and I knew that many of the very conservative individuals who made up St. Johnsbury's Democratic Town Committee had opposed the civil union law and hadn't been happy with my support of it.

I decided to submit a petition to run for JP as a Democrat without having been officially nominated by the Democratic committee. Sheila Reed, secretary of the town committee, Bob South, chairman of the county Democratic committee, and Stephanie Churchill, a longtime and devoted Democratic Party worker, had all also been rejected in the nominating process and decided to submit their own nominating petitions as well.

This brought down the wrath of many upon our heads, including, of course, the *Caledonian-Record,* which never missed an opportunity to criticize me. In an editorial the paper suggested I resign my post as the

Democratic Town Committee chair since I was going to run as an independent, an incorrect statement of fact. Other articles and letters to the editor referred to the four of us as "power grabbers" challenging the "old guard." The headlines, however, were pointed at me: "Shame on Yessne," the paper declared, and "Yessne needs to rethink the values," it admonished.

It wasn't too surprising that the Democrats who had been nominated at the caucus kept carefully quiet, as that was in their best interest if they wanted to be elected. I was startled, however, when the St. Johnsbury Republicans decided that this was their fight too, and began an all-out effort to make sure I wasn't successful in my bid to keep my JP seat. It increased my suspicion that the attempt to expel me from the ranks of JPs was a result of my very strong and public support of the civil union legislation in 2000, and the fact that I had officiated at many civil unions since.

As election day approached, I really had no idea how things would turn out, but I was cautiously optimistic.

Then, on the Wednesday before election day—too late for me to respond according to the paper's self-imposed deadline—the *Caledonian* published a long letter full of lies about me. The writer accused the four of us of breaking the sixty-year tradition of the gentlemen's agreement after "explicitly endorsing [it] on August 27th at our caucus," and "breaking our word" by filing independently when it was too late for Republicans and Democrats to reconvene and each nominate a full slate of candidates. This was too much for me, as I had many friends in the community whose politics were different than mine but who still respected me, and I wasn't happy at being falsely and publicly accused of breaking my word.

At the time of the August 27 caucus I'd been hundreds of miles away from St. Johnsbury, and whether anyone else had explicitly endorsed the gentlemen's agreement or anything else that evening, which I doubted, nothing had been endorsed by me. With response in hand I marched into the publisher's office and demanded that policy or no policy, my letter rebutting the attack be published prior to election day. If it wasn't, I said, the paper would find itself in serious trouble. Since the paper had been following every step of the story very closely, I said, it surely must have known, or should have known, that I wasn't even present at the caucus and that it was publishing lies about me.

My letter appeared on Monday, pointing out one by one each lie or misrepresentation of the truth that had been penned. When the votes were counted the next day, I had won one of the fifteen JP positions, defeating the next candidate in line by almost 200 votes.

*   *   *

I had been working from home for some time prior to passage of the civil union legislation and all that ensued, mostly on SSI disability cases and my quasi-judicial work for the secretary of state. In 2002 I added a new piece of work. As a consequence of the Master Settlement Agreement entered into between the major tobacco companies and most of the states, the Vermont attorney general's office was building a tobacco unit within its Division of Public Protection, and was looking for a part-time attorney to ride herd on the predominantly small, foreign tobacco companies who had not signed the agreement, but who, by its terms, were subject to a number of legal and financial requirements that had been established and were required to be "diligently enforced" by the state. Since nearly all of the work was done by mail, email, and conference calls, I was able to negotiate an appointment that allowed me to work from home most of the time and to continue to do my Social Security disability work.

The arrangement worked for me and worked for the AG's office. I had little need to consult with anyone in person and maintained what was virtually a zero-tolerance level of noncompliance by the tobacco manufacturers I was monitoring. I would remain in the job for five years and it proved to be the last legal job I held. The fruits of my labors paid off in 2018 when the State of Vermont was awarded $28 million in the settlement of a multistate lawsuit with the major tobacco companies, based largely on the work I had done years before.

On the Arcosanti cafe balcony, 2005
Courtesy of Sandra Wayne

That's me with the hose
Courtesy of the Cosanti Foundation

Our skyline apartment at Arcosanti (far right) overlooking the Amphitheatre
Courtesy of the Cosanti Foundation.

Chapter Thirteen
Searching for Home
2003-2007

Paolo Soleri had been one of my early heroes when I lived in New York City and started thinking about the connections between dance therapy and architecture. I hadn't thought much about him or those ideas since I'd moved to Vermont in 1970 and proceeded in a different direction with my life. But in late 1992, on a visit to Arizona with my family, I had spotted a sign for Arcosanti, Solari's real-life experiment in urban design—and insisted that we turn in and take a look.

Everyone's jaw drops when they first see Arcosanti, and for me it was no different. I felt as though I was eight years old again and someone had just dropped me into a Flash Gordon comic book to begin living in the future. We were there under an hour, not even time to take a tour, but the soaring expanse of the main building, the incredible views from the arcology—the built site at the top of the mesa—and the unusual design of every structure I could see was indelibly etched in my mind. I knew I had to go back and explore it further.

The following year when Daniel and I went to Arizona for our second PIT project in the spring of 1993, I allowed us an extra day for sightseeing and we drove up to Arcosanti to have another look. Daniel had also been quite taken with the place the first time we were there, and as usual was up for anything that promised an opportunity to explore new territory. I don't remember exactly how we spent the day, only that my first impression of it as an extraordinary place I wanted to know more about was confirmed; then other things pushed it to the back of my mind again for nearly a decade.

Why I went surfing on the internet in late 2002 to find Arcosanti again I do not remember. With winter on the way, perhaps my thoughts had simply turned to previous spring trips to Arizona in search of a break from the lingering ice and snow in Vermont. Or, perhaps it was on the rebound from my second attempt to secure a Vermont judgeship.

This time I'd had no trouble convincing the Judicial Nominating Board that I was worthy of having my name forwarded to the governor for consideration. My legal work on the *MMWEC* case, on the Vermont Labor Relations Board, and as an appellate officer for the secretary of state—in addition to my earlier advocacy work within the bar—had brought me to the favorable attention of those in the legal establishment who now comprised the board. But Howard Dean was still governor, and not much time had passed since I'd castigated him in VLIAC's *ACTION ALERT*s for his insensitivity to the problems of the poor; after an uninspired interview on both our parts, I wasn't surprised when I wasn't appointed.

Once online I discovered that the Cosanti Foundation offered six-week educational workshops at Arcosanti open to anyone regardless of background. I was immediately attracted to the possibility. Here was a way I could indulge my long-standing interest in architecture, which had broadened through my work on my cabin at Mad Brook Farm to include the process of construction, without leaving my real job.

I sent off my letter and received word back that I was accepted for the March 2003 workshop. The AG's office approved my leave on the condition that I maintain contact and continue to participate in any conference calls scheduled while I would be gone. I was happy to agree to this, for I knew not what I was getting into, and thought that keeping myself anchored to my job was probably a good thing and would give me a sense of security if the adventure turned sour.

I flew to Phoenix, boarded a shuttle van to Cordes Junction, and arrived there in midafternoon along with a young man from Tokyo named Shunitchi, who turned out to be a fellow workshop participant. He was three years out of college and not sure what he wanted to do next; an architect friend in Japan had suggested he check the place out. We piled into the waiting Volvo with all the worldly goods we each had thought we'd need to get by in the middle of nowhere for six weeks, and headed down the dusty road with Wes, the workshop coordinator.

As we proceeded down the road Wes said he was planning on putting me in one of the guest rooms, but as we drove past them I wasn't sure I liked the idea. The guest rooms are built into the hillside and have a spectacular view, and I figured they were probably a little larger and nicer than the rooms assigned to the workshoppers, but they are isolated from both the arcology at the top of the mesa, and from "Camp" at the bottom of the mesa, where I guessed most of the action would take place. I didn't want to make waves before I'd even unpacked, but I could see that things weren't going in the right direction; I said I didn't need a guest room and would be happy to be in Camp if there was room for me.

Camp is the area where the first wave of Arcosanti volunteers lived in the 1960s when they were beginning construction of the arcology up the hill. Of immediate interest to me was that it looked and felt exactly like that part of Kibbutz Urim where they housed *their* workshoppers—the young people who came from Canada and the States to live and work for a year. The kibbutz figured that being young and not used to frills or conveniences yet, the volunteers would be happy enough in the older, funkier housing. This also seemed to be the hope of Arcosanti. The parallel was striking: the use of the same word for the "workshoppers," and the same funky, dilapidated housing surrounded by dusty roads and paths almost uncanny. I immediately felt at home.

The only available rooms were in the bunkhouse, a wooden structure of fourteen little rooms, seven in a row facing the center of Camp, and seven back to back with them, facing the creek bed. In addition to a few human inhabitants who were busying themselves, there were various species of chickens, ducks, peacocks, and emus lurking close by, as Camp was also the location of Arcosanti's farm. It was quickly apparent that Camp was going to be a lot more interesting than the guest rooms.

I chose a room at the end of the bunkhouse on the side overlooking the creek bed, which had only a dribble of water in it. I chose it because it had a desk and a chair, and I knew I was going to have some work to do. The room was just 8' x 8', but the ceiling sloped up to a height of about 10' in the back where the roof peaked, and the side facing the river had both a clear Plexiglas door and a window, making it feel a little larger than it was.

In addition to the desk and chair there was a "bed," a piece of plywood on wooden legs with a 4"-thick piece of well-used foam on top. Previous tenants had left some items behind: a very handy little triangular shelf in a corner by the window; a handmade wooden cup half-filled with shells and feathers; a wreath of dried grasses and flowers; a rather odd abstract painting of something resembling a sunflower; a tiny plastic toy scythe; and two 8 ½" x 11" prints that I didn't like at all and immediately removed, replacing them with the March and April pages from a current calendar and a nice picture of Jim and the dogs that I had taken before I left.

Settling in, I hung two strings of little white lights I had brought to cheer myself up if I needed cheering, spread my colorful Mexican blanket on the bed, stuffed most of my work clothes in the one functioning drawer that remained in the desk, and left my "good" clothes in my small suitcase at the foot of the bed. All my little bottles and tubes went on the triangular shelf and, on the desk, into an empty clementine box I had brought for just this purpose and placed next to my Bodum tea kettle, went my tea bags, hot cocoa mix, and four tiny bottles of cheap Merlot that I had bought in the Phoenix airport. The overall effect was excellent and I felt quite content.

This business of what makes a space feel like home, and how people furnish their homes, is of great interest to me and something I think about often. It seems as if the homes that are the most comfortable to be in are the ones that are full of stuff—the things that have been left out or placed around to remind the people who live there of happy or significant times in their lives. In that most personal of my living spaces, my cabin at Mad Brook Farm, furnished without having to consider anyone else's wants or needs, that has certainly been the case. As the late Gloria Vanderbilt once said, "decorating is autobiography."[29] I couldn't agree with her more.

*   *   *

The first week at Arcosanti, Seminar Week, gave me a philosophical basis for understanding Soleri's work, acquainted me with the highly unusual physical layout of the place and the mixed uses of Arcosanti's buildings, and a taste of the work done by each of the departments. As we were introduced to administrators, department heads, and of course Paolo Soleri himself, and met other residents at meals in the cafe, I realized that in addition to being part of a very unusual experiment in architecture and city planning, I was now also part of an international community, with many Italian, Japansese, and Brazilian architecture and city-planning students in particular, living on site. I also continued to appreciate just

---

[29] Penelope Green, "Gloria Vanderbilt's Story (Reprised)," *New York Times,* April 2, 2016.

how much like a kibbutz Arcosanti felt, since I had enjoyed that construct so much when I lived in Israel. The feeling came from once again being in a compact residential pedestrian community where all the parts of my present life were in walking distance of each other and automobiles relegated to a perimeter road and unseen in the course of a day.

At the end of Seminar Week I joined the construction department for the remaining five weeks of work experience under the supervision of a very matter-of-fact but humorous man named Ray Shong. An experienced contractor, Shong was overseeing the continuing construction of Arcosanti's largest structure, the East Crescent. The crew he was putting together included both permanent residents and workshoppers, who would be undertaking the pour of the third floor on the north side of the Crescent.

The next five weeks literally cemented my love of the southwest and my positive feelings about the great experiment Soleri was conducting. I learned to cut rebar with a hand grinder, tie the rebar grid together with plastic strips, support the grid with little plastic platforms at each intersection, and pour and screed concrete, all of which were skills I knew full well I would never use again. However, I also got pretty good on the table and chop saws, and learned to use the laser level, which we used to check the second-floor supports. We started work early in the morning each day, as we were working unsheltered in the hot Arizona sun.

All too soon I had to return to my work at the attorney general's office, but I found it difficult to get Arcosanti out of my mind. The truth is, that even after so many years, Vermont had never really felt like home to me, and part of me was perpetually wondering if there wasn't somewhere else I was meant to be. Those born and raised in rural Vermont know a very different world than I do, and those who have moved to Vermont and stayed have largely self-selected themselves to fit into that isolated, rural existence. In my case Vermont was an adventure when I was young, but as I became a mature adult and found myself wanting something more, I have sometimes had a very hard time accepting my place here. In my worst moments, the thought of being buried for all time in the St. Johnsbury cemetery filled me with dread.

So, when I was invited to be part of the Centennial PIT Project at Kentucky Camp in early 2004, I jumped at the chance to go back to Arizona and take a closer look at the archaeological and arcological worlds I'd become a part of there.

One morning when things were slow to get going, a friend and I took a long hike on the Arizona trail that led out of Kentucky Camp, reaching the top of a ridge where we were treated to a 360-degree view for many miles in every direction. One of the things I like most about Arizona, and which is so different from Vermont, is that wherever you are you can usually see a great distance, and so have a sense of where you are in relation to both where you've been and where you're going. This vastness is one of the things that continues to draw me to the desert. I think it's important to have a sense of yourself in relation to the rest of the world as a way of keeping things in perspective, and what follows from that is a certain humility, a trait I admire in others and strive for in myself.

At the end of the week's PIT project I headed north to Arcosanti for a visit. I had an ulterior motive, which was to see what I could find out about what it was like to live there for an extended period of time. I'd been thinking since I'd left the year before that this was something I might like to do, but Jim kept reminding me that when I'd been there on my workshop there had been plenty of things I didn't like about the place, at least as he had gleaned them from my emails at the time. In this he was quite right. I had enjoyed my work experience and the field trips, but I did find the evenings and weekends quite difficult and more than a little lonely. It seemed that after work, and certainly after dinner for the small number of older people who ate in the cafe, everyone just disappeared. I'd gone looking for them in what I thought were the likely places, but never found them. I could only assume they had retreated to their own apartments, and no one had invited me to join them.

Although it made me unhappy at the time, it also made sense to me that the older adult population who were my peers had paid so little attention to me. From the point of view of a permanent resident, there's really not much reason to invest a lot of time and energy on the workshop people who come and go every six weeks. In the last week of my workshop, however, a few of the older residents had suddenly started talking to me and asking if I might be staying on. At the time this rather startled me. I had always assumed that the workshop was a short-term educational experience from which all of the participants would return to real life at the end of six weeks. The question seemed to suggest that it could also be a launching pad for a radically different life. I hadn't realized that people came for a workshop intending to stay on, but actually living at Arcosanti was an intriguing idea. I was looking forward to having some conversations with women my age about what it was like to live there as a more or less permanent resident.

As I walked around, I could see that the place hadn't changed much in a year. One has to be patient with Arcosanti, because it's being built by volunteers who are learning as they go, and things proceed at a snail's pace. It's an inordinately inefficient place as far as that goes, but then again, more than 8,000 people have taken the workshops and lent a hand while learning about Soleri's philosophy of life and city planning at the same time. As an educational foundation, it was certainly meeting its goals.

The first person I found who I wanted to talk to was Valkiri. Valkiri is my age, a ceramicist who had led a tile workshop I had enjoyed during the last week of my workshop. She was very encouraging about my coming back, but suggested I come for three months the next time to see how I liked it.

Then I caught up with Shirlee, Arcosanti's eighty-year-old no-nonsense office manager and receptionist. Among the things that had drawn me to her were her excellent customer service skills, which seemed delightfully out of place at this odd community, aptly described by Soleri as an inhabited construction site. I was especially interested in talking to her because she had come to Arcosanti at the age of sixty-five and for all outward appearances had stayed there quite contentedly for the next sixteen years. We ended up talking for over three hours, about what life was like there for her, how the place was being run, and what the current issues were. She, too, was very encouraging about my coming back again, and also recommended a three-month stay to see how I liked it.

Shirlee was a member of the six-person Arcosanti Leadership Team, commonly referred to as "ALT." One of the things they had been discussing, she told me, was the need for personnel policies, of which they had none. This was a little shocking to me, but given what little I'd learned already about how the place was run, not really surprising once I thought about it. When I told her that labor law was one of my areas of interest and expertise she got quite excited, and I learned the next day that as soon as I left she began making phone calls to some key people telling them how great it would be if I came back to help with the personnel policies.

I headed back to Phoenix feeling that I did want to help Arcosanti if I could, and that if it could be arranged, I would like to go back for three months. I thought it would be interesting to see if personnel policies could be developed that would raise the level of responsibility and accountability among Arcosanti's employees without losing what was so unusual and special about the place and what made them willing to work there for so little money. At the same time, I thought I would get an in-depth understanding of the community that would help me avoid the mistakes I had made when I moved the family to Oregon.

*   *   *

My return to Arcosanti didn't happen for yet another year, but in early 2005 the AG's office agreed to give me a three-month leave of absence on the condition that I stay up to date with my tobacco settlement email and conference calls, and in good enough touch with the office to deal with any emergencies that might come up. Since I would have a cubicle with a desk and a phone in Arcosanti's main office this time around, I saw no difficulty with that and agreed.

I spent the first three months of 2005 in residence at Arcosanti, doing my work for the attorney general's office after my Arcosanti workday ended. My task was to draft personnel policies for the Cosanti Foundation, the entity that employs everyone at Arcosanti other than those working for Cosanti Originals, Inc., the for-profit endeavor that oversees the foundry and ceramics, where the famous Soleri bells are produced, as well as the bakery, cafe, and visitor center. I was made a member of ALT as a way of keeping the leadership up to date on my work and encouraging their ongoing feedback. I interviewed department heads, supervisors, and employees, in short anyone who would talk to me about what was working well at Arcosanti from an employment point of view, and what wasn't. At the end of the three months I provided ALT with a draft personnel manual, leaving it to them to discuss, finalize, and implement.

My other task, of course, had been to figure out if Arcosanti was a place I might want to live, and if so, how that would work for Jim and the kids. By this time both children were out of the house and I was pretty sure that neither one had any thought of moving into our home again on a permanent basis. But on the other hand, any mention of the possibility that Jim and I might live somewhere other than in the house where they'd grown up had always triggered a protest. As for Jim, he would be seventy-five in June and had been working only part time for years. Chances were he was ready to retire, something I thought he could do at Arcosanti as well as anywhere else.

The big issue seemed to be money. If Jim quit his job and we moved to Arcosanti we'd be able to get by on the meager $8.50/hour I'd get there plus his Social Security, but if it didn't work out the chance of his getting a job again somewhere else was slim. So it called for careful evaluation.

The interviews I conducted were very helpful. Assured of confidentiality, no one was shy in telling me all the things they thought were wrong with Arcosanti without limiting their comments to employment issues. Getting to know the management team gave me a good sense of where the place was heading, at what pace, and what kind of a contribution I might be able to make.

Jim flew out for a visit in February. As I was staying in the guest rooms for this three-month period, he moved right in with me. I took him around to all my favorite places and places I hadn't seen but thought he'd like. Everyone greeted him warmly and generally he formed a favorable impression.

By the end of the three months I'd decided that I wanted to return again for a longer look. Based on my observations about where attention was needed and my personal inclination as to where I thought I would enjoy making a contribution, Site Coordinator Mary Hoadley and I developed a position called director of guest services and on-site tourism. I would take over the general areas of visitor customer service, tour-guide training and scheduling, maintenance and improvement of guest rooms, and scheduling and accommodation of visiting groups. I said I'd be back in the fall and offered to make some workshop recruitment visits to colleges on my way out. Armed with print materials and a CD on Arcosanti, I returned to Vermont, gave my notice to the attorney general's office, and began to put my Vermont affairs in order. Jim would remain in our house and at his part-time job until we knew how things were going to work out.

*   *   *

I headed west again at the beginning of September 2005. I had arranged recruiting visits to Cornell, Ithaca College, and Oberlin on my way out, and these all went very well, particularly at Oberlin, where Daniel was starting his senior year and drummed up a good crowd for me. I've always enjoyed working with young people, and those I met at the three colleges were no exception. I was in a very good mood when I arrived back at Arcosanti, and my mood improved even further when I learned where I would be living.

A young couple, both architects and permanent residents, were on leave with their young son for a year at Auroville, Arcosanti's sister community in India. Their home was one of the most unusual and beautiful residences at Arcosanti, and together with an adjacent apartment that was its mirror image, ringed the back side of the foundry to form an apse. The couple had given a Brazilian woman and her boyfriend permission to live in the apartment while they were away, but that left available a spacious room on the canyon end of the apartment that had been serving as the son's bedroom, but had been built as a separate unit with its own tiny bathroom and an exterior door, and could temporarily be returned to that state very easily. I was to be the lucky one to get it for my residence.

Smack dab in the middle of all the action, a stone's throw from Crafts III, the building that housed the cafe, bakery, visitor's center, and several apartments, and across a small lawn from the ceramics apse, my room was on everyone's way to everywhere. At the head of the bed was a large rectangular window that looked out into the foundry, and on the end wall was a large round window perhaps five feet in diameter, looking south out over the canyon to the mesa on the other side. The natural light was lovely, and the view stunning. An easy stop for people coming and going from Crafts III, I finally started to get to know the people my age—particularly the women—and made some good friends.

As my first order of business, I took on the upgrading of the guest rooms, the run of eleven small rooms below the swimming pool and overlooking the canyon; and the Sky Suite, Arcosanti's premier guest accommodation at the top of the East Crescent. The guest rooms were priced at a very low rate, and it was no wonder. Although each boasted a lovely silt cast design in its ceiling and a front wall entirely of glass overlooking the canyon, that was the end of their positive features. The beds were all old iron army beds, and the only other furniture was a small slant-top desk and wooden chair. There were no closets and nowhere else to put clothing or personal possessions that couldn't survive a slide to the floor.

The Sky Suite had more amenities and had clearly received a little more attention. It was strikingly designed on four levels, and consisted of two bedrooms with built-in closets and other storage; a reasonably sized bathroom; and an open living space that included a kitchenette, a built-in table with two stools and a chair, and a loveseat. The walls of the main living space were glass on three sides that soared upward to a cathedral ceiling. But the Sky Suite also had problems: window coverings were stained and torn or didn't work right. The loveseat had seen better days. A random assortment of pots and pans suggested that no one would really want to cook there anyway.

I knew that money was always tight at Arcosanti, and that there would be little to spare for an upgrade of furnishings in these rooms that Paolo apparently cared so little about, so I tried to make my requests as minimal as possible. Fortunately, Mary realized just how bad things were and trusted me to improve them as inexpensively as I could. Having had an extended stay in a guest room during my previous time at Arcosanti, I knew what had to be done.

With completion of the upgrades the rates were raised to a whopping $25/night for a single-occupancy room with shared bath, and up to $45/night for a double-occupancy room with private bath, all room fees including breakfast. It may have been the best overnight deal in the entire state of Arizona.

My favorite part of the guest services job was doing group tours of Arcosanti for special groups. The most common were groups of architecture, urban design, or urban-planning students, from places as nearby as Prescott College or as far away as Italy, Scandinavia, or Japan; but there were many other groups drawn to the place for entertainment, or diversion, or just out of curiosity. Some knew of Paolo's work and were anxious to meet him, and came on Wednesday to attend his weekly seminar. Others couldn't have cared less about Paolo but were looking for an enjoyable afternoon: a tour, a good, reasonably priced lunch, and "one of those bells" that the foundry and ceramics produced for sale. The Red Hat Society ladies of Prescott Valley might show up one day, and the next day a middle-school group from down near the Mexican border might make us a stop on their geology field trip, and so it went.

Most groups of any size thoughtfully called ahead. I appreciated this so I could warn the cafe and bakery in order not to run out of food.

I also appreciated it because it meant that I could schedule myself to lead any tour groups that were of particular interest to me. I found it an enjoyable challenge to customize a tour to the background and interests of the participants, which made it far more valuable to them and a far more interesting time for me. Two groups that remain vivid in my mind even after all these years are the rabbis and the neon-sign makers.

The rabbis were staying in Phoenix while attending a national rabbinical convention. One of them, who knew a little bit about Paolo and Arcosanti already, had convinced five or six others to join him in a sojourn north when they found themselves with a free afternoon. We started out covering all of the usual tour information, but as we got to know each other and I discovered a personal connection with one of them, our conversation expanded into a wide-ranging discussion of one of my favorite topics: how people use space, and how much space people think they need to use.

All of the rabbis had spent time in Israel, which gave us a common basis for discussion. We marveled at how most kibbutzniks, like the Arcosanti residents living in very small quarters, nonetheless have as high a standard of living as a middle-class American, and all the same conveniences: dishwashers, sound systems, computers, etc. The rabbis contrasted this with what they saw on visits to the homes of their more affluent congregants, where the "great hall" inside the front door might typically provide more floor space than an entire kibbutz living unit for a family of four, yet serve no real purpose.

Visitors to Arcosanti are always very curious about the residential spaces but see none of them on the tour. So I always made sure when I was leaving for a tour I had high hopes for, that our apartment was in order; then I could add it as a stop to show them what an Arcosanti living unit actually looked like. The rabbis were one of those groups.

The neon-sign makers were a different sort altogether. There were about sixty of them in all, from a company in Las Vegas that had chosen Arcosanti for its annual company outing, to give them something a little different from the Las Vegas strip for inspiration. They had scheduled an entire day's visit, including a tour, lunch, a silt cast demonstration, and a private meeting in the late afternoon with Paolo. I had a third of them on my tour, and delighted in how refreshing and uncontrived they found the Arcosanti environment, fantasizing as many do when they visit about how great it would be to live there. I had wondered how Paolo would relate to them, since on the surface they seemed to have little in common. I ought not to have worried. Using "light" as the theme for his talk at their private meeting, he spoke eloquently about his use of the sun's natural light in urban design and their use of neon signs to some of the same ends. They were charmed.

The overnight groups presented greater challenges and much more work, if only because of the number of extra beds I had to come up with, which could go as high as thirty or more. In these cases, we cleared out classrooms and meeting rooms and any other rooms that could be spared, hauled in folding beds and mattresses, and sometimes just put mats on the floor. These groups were my responsibility, which meant sharing in the heavy lifting, making all the beds, developing a schedule for the time they would be on site, and notifying the departments that would be affected, if not actively engaged with the participants.

To the credit of every resident of Arcosanti and especially the department heads, there was rarely any grumbling about the need to adjust their own plans and activities to the needs of these groups, even though that often meant delaying projects, upending schedules, and always, extra work. Everyone knew that the income from these groups helped keep the place afloat, and that was enough to make it work.

From September 2005 until June 2006 I was focused entirely on my work. I went home to Vermont in December for Christmas, and had a good visit. In March, Jim came out to Arcosanti again, and this time stayed with me in my one-room apartment overlooking the foundry, and had to agree that Arcosanti housing was pretty unusual in its ability to combine beauty and comfort with frugality. I introduced him to quite a few people I knew well by then, and by the time he left we had decided to make a move to Arcosanti and give it a try. I was very excited about our plans and began collecting and squirreling away anything I came across that I thought might be useful to us in creating a home there.

In June I flew back to Vermont, rented our house out for a year, and together with Jim once again headed cross country in tandem with a U-Haul truck and our car, this time with our dog Rufus and our cat Alice. We arrived back at Arcosanti on July 15 and moved into a highly coveted apartment on the top floor of the East Crescent, which Mary had assigned to us. It was a beautiful split-level studio apartment that had never been lived in. It looked out over the East Crescent, the amphitheatre, and across the canyon.

The apartment, and the accommodation made for Rufus, were two tremendous gifts to us from Mary. By Paolo's long-standing edict, dogs were not allowed at Arcosanti, but we had made it clear we weren't willing to come without him. So we were delighted to learn when we arrived that Paul Vigne, Arcosanti's purchasing agent, who lived in an old ranch house on an untraveled section of Arcosanti's property, had agreed to take him in as a foster dog. Because of his age Jim would only be working half time once he finished his workshop, so he was free to head down to visit Rufus each afternoon and hang out with him while he chased rabbits.

It turned out to be a fine arrangement. Paul and Rufus hit it off from the start, and we managed to smuggle Rufus up the hill and into our apartment on weekends for special attention and to give Paul a break. Rufus also managed to escape to the built site now and then, but he kept out of any serious trouble for the most part. Jim and Paul worked together fencing in an enclosure for Rufus at Paul's house, and in the process developed a relationship that I think enhanced the social life of both.

As happy as Rufus and I were with our situations, however, Jim was not happy with his. He had a part-time job in the archives which he enjoyed very much, and he learned a tremendous amount about the interesting history of Arcosanti in the process, but he found Arcosanti to be a singularly unfriendly place for someone his age, and most of the residents impossible to relate to. To this day, when someone asks him how he liked it there, he recounts how he would walk across the site from the archives to the cafe, passing fellow residents of all ages, who would—to a person—fail to respond to his smile and hello with any sign of life, let alone friendliness.

Other than Paolo, who was eighty-three at the time and only on site occasionally, as his primary residence was at Cosanti, in Scottsdale, and Shirlee, who was right behind Paolo in age, Jim was the only other person in that age category. Once a week when we got back from meetings of ALT, Shirlee, Jim, and I took to splitting a bottle of wine in our apartment before dinner, where we would enjoy ridding ourselves of the week's frustrations. But overall Arcosanti was an unpleasant existence for Jim, and when May rolled around and our Vermont tenants purchased a home of their own, he was happy to go back to his garden for the summer, as we had agreed he would.

About halfway through the summer Jim announced that he didn't want to return to Arcosanti, leaving us with the choice of returning to live in Vermont full time or going somewhere else. Going somewhere else and starting over again seemed like more than I wanted to take on, and I felt I had little choice but to return to Vermont. I was angry and didn't want to call a halt to this great experiment we had embarked on, but Jim could not be swayed and we simply couldn't afford to live in two places.

2018 Vermont Poor People's Campaign
Montpelier, Vermont
Courtesy of Erin Rose

State Street Civil Disobedience
Montpelier, Vermont, June 4, 2018
Courtesy of Erin Rose

Vermont Statehouse Sit-in
Montpelier, Vermont, May 21, 2018
Courtesy VTDigger

Statehouse Campaign Rally
Montpelier, Vermont, January 20, 2018
Courtesy of Vermont Poor People's Campaign

Chapter Fourteen

You Don't Need to Be Famous to Make Things Better

—Aaron Henry

2008-2018

I started sending out letters of inquiry once it became clear that we'd be returning to St. Johnsbury, but there weren't many jobs to apply for and I found it hard to get excited about any of them when my heart was still at Arcosanti.

Once we had returned in late 2007, several people mentioned to me that the Community Justice Center was looking for a new director. That seemed a step backward that I didn't want to take, until I ran into Town Manager Mike Welch on the street one day and he urged me to reconsider.

The relationship between the town and the CJC had changed, Welch said, with the town now taking an ownership interest in the program and the staff becoming town employees with benefits. An independent board made up of private individuals still had authority to determine program and policy. I followed up with several friends who were volunteering at the CJC, and encouraged by what I heard, applied for the job and became the director once again.

Some of my best work during my second tenure at the CJC was our development and nurturing of four neighborhood associations in the town, an effort that had Welch's strong backing as well as that of my board.

Neighborhood organizations have a proven record as a protective factor against crime, which pleased both our funders at the Vermont Department of Corrections as well as the St. Johnsbury Police Department. But in addition, neighborhood organizations are more generally a means of strengthening communities and improving the quality of life for the people who live in them, and this was of particular interest to me, because soon after I started work at the CJC again a staunchly regressive selectboard took over, forced Welch's resignation, and hired an unknown newcomer in his place.

Ralph Nelson was a Major League Baseball administrator who, by all accounts, just happened to be passing through town with his wife on a pilgrimage to Stephen Huneck's Dog Mountain. He heard about the job opening and decided to stay, apply for the town manager's job, and save the town from itself. Our rather provincial selectboard was impressed by his background and hired him, then allowed him to run things into the ground, making the town the butt of jokes around the state.

As *Vermont Digger* described it, "even before Welch quit, the economic development director's job had been abolished and the zoning administrator resigned after her position was downgraded. It wasn't long before several other senior town officials—the police chief, the fire chief, the assistant clerk, and more—were forced out of office, or resigned or abruptly retired. Since then, town government has not been a happy camp."[30]

I was not a senior town official by any means, but working for the town had become difficult and disturbing for me, too, and I decided to retire in 2012. Things had come to a head when I failed to receive reimbursement for my January and February health care costs and was unable to find out why despite repeated inquiries. It turned out that the town's fiscal office was almost totally dysfunctional due to the resignations of both the town clerk

---

[30] Jon Margolis, "The St. Johnsbury Follies," *Vermont Digger,* December 26, 2012.

and treasurer and the assistant town clerk within a week of each other. No one left in the town office could find any of the CJC's financial information, grants, contracts, or other governing documents, and Nelson, for whom the CJC was the first grant-funded program he'd ever dealt with, didn't have a clue where to look or what to do about it. Despite my repeated attempts to work things out both with and without the help of the town attorney, it became clear that there remained nothing to do but sue for the more than $2,100 that the town owed me. I retired in May, glad to be out of there.

The director of Umbrella had a couple of ideas about how I could fill my time once I left town employment. She had decided to run for the state legislature from St. Johnsbury and asked for my help, which I was happy to give. Everyone thought I was her campaign manager, but that was just me working as hard as I could to elect her, which we did in November 2012.

At the time Umbrella was exploring the possibility of starting a culinary arts training program for women in transition, and now that its director was going to be in Montpelier all winter and spring the agency needed someone else to do a feasibility study for the proposed program, and, if indicated, draw up a business plan. I took on the project and stayed with it through the hiring of Cornucopia's first director in July 2013.

Happily retired, I was determined to get back to using my hands as well as my head, and since Jim had by now passed his 80th birthday, I wondered if it wasn't time to start looking for a smaller place in town that I could fix up and rent to others until we were ready to make a move ourselves. My interest in architecture had never waned, and my years of working on my cabin at Mad Brook Farm, along with my construction experience at Arcosanti, had given me the confidence to take on a major renovation. I set out to see what there was in town that might work for us when we needed it, and in the meantime be a source of income.

The house I came across in St. Johnsbury did not meet my criteria. It was a two-story duplex and it certainly needed fixing up. But getting to the first floor required hiking up a steep set of concrete stairs from street level, as the house sat atop its street-level basement/garage. At eighty, and with one leg already weak from childhood polio, Jim found managing the outside steps difficult, and in time, perhaps, might not be able to manage them at all.

But the house intrigued me. It was one of two houses that sat next to each other, built as mirror images. The view from both residential floors was interesting, looking out, over, and beyond the municipal parking lot to the historic buildings on Railroad Street, and behind them to rolling hills.

I made an offer on the building and negotiated with the owner for a time, before we reached a stalemate and he decided to take it off the market. I continued to look at other places without finding anything quite right, but I never forgot the duplex. When it came back on the market about a year later, I repeated my last offer and the owner accepted it, and soon I was off and running with a property to renovate.

I worked on the house for a year and a half, first finishing the upstairs so I could rent it and have some money coming in, then moving on to the downstairs. I learned to repair plaster; cut, tape, and mud drywall; lay flooring; install wainscoting; disconnect and replace sinks; tile shower stalls, floors, and backsplashes; and do many other things. I had a routine for approaching tasks that I'd never done before, which was pretty much everything: I would read up to ten internet versions of how to do whatever task it was that I was facing, choose the one that gave the clearest directions and print it out, add any helpful hints from the other versions, and then carefully proceed step by step. This worked amazingly well. Whenever I ran up against anything I couldn't understand or manage by myself I turned to a friend whose work I admired and was always pleased with the result.

Unfortunately, I never found the St. Johnsbury house I was looking for that Jim and I could move into, so when it became clear that our Goss Hollow house had finally become more than we wanted to deal with, I started looking instead in the direction of Calais, where Daniel and his wife Adrian had settled. I didn't want to infringe on their independence, but thought that being closer to them could only be of mutual benefit to two young people working full time, trying to rehabilitate an old farmhouse, and expecting a baby; as well as to an older couple who weren't quite ready to give up home ownership, but were becoming less and less willing and able to deal with all it entails.

We found the place we wanted and in late autumn of 2016 closed on a renovated one-room schoolhouse in Adamant, a community with no particular borders that includes residents of Calais, like us, and residents of East Montpelier as well. As we got to know the community we came to understand the basis of the local adage, "if you think you live in Adamant, you do." From the start there seemed to be something special about this little hamlet where life revolves around a food co-op founded in 1935 and still in its original building.

Calais is a progressive community politically, and it was vastly reassuring to arrive there on November 1 to see campaign signs for people I knew or knew of, who were part of Vermont's progressive political scene. A week later, when Donald Trump was elected president, I was even happier we had made the move. In addition to the progressive vibe in Calais, Central Vermont seemed to be bursting with organizations addressing important political and social justice issues. The question was, where did I want to put my time and energy?

I soon learned that Calais had an Indivisible chapter. Formed after Trump's election to resist his agenda, the parent organization has been described as an "antidote to despair."[31] The Calais group consisted of a small group of women who met regularly, and a larger group of people who could

---

[31]Casey Tolan, "Meet the Husband-Wife Duo Who Are Sparking a Liberal Tea Party Movement," San Jose *Mercury News,* May 13, 2017.

be counted on to come forward when needed. The group's commitment to the Resistance was unquestionable, and their energy level astoundingly high, but their emphasis was on fundraising and postcard writing for candidates in other states, and that was not quite the interaction I was looking for.

I checked out several other political groups in the area, but none seemed particularly welcoming of an older white retiree who was unknown to them. In fact, the more I looked the more it seemed to me that these organizations had each become a rather homogeneous silo unto itself. I tried to understand this in the context of history, but as a coalition builder and movement type, it made me feel useless and rather sad.

Toward the fall of 2017 I heard about the revival of the Poor People's Campaign and it caught my interest. I knew that Dr. Martin Luther King Jr., just prior to his assassination in 1968, had enlarged his work from a focus on civil rights to a broader assault on the economic forces driving racism, poverty, and the war in Vietnam, and had called that new effort the Poor People's Campaign. The campaign had been gathering momentum and was headed for a major encampment and demonstration in Washington, D.C. to demand new anti-poverty legislation when King was gunned down in Memphis. With Robert Kennedy's assassination two months later, and then the riots surrounding the 1968 Democratic Convention in August, the campaign never regained its drive as a stunned nation tried to recover from the events of the year, many by dropping out entirely.

Now, the new leadership of the Poor People's Campaign had issued a national call for moral revival, and had added climate change and ecological devastation to the list of urgent and interrelated problems, calling on people concerned with any of them to come forward again and rebuild the movement.

I had been attracted to the original Poor People's Campaign, had attended one of its rallies in Washington, and was more than a little interested in the possibility of its revival. I particularly welcomed the idea of organizing across issues again, as I have always felt them to be fundamentally connected and the task of bringing their activists together the only way to build a movement strong enough to make real and lasting change.

Finding the Vermont chapter on the internet, I attended an informational meeting in the fall of 2017 and liked what I heard, so I joined up and was there when the Vermont Poor People's Campaign held its kickoff event at the Vermont Statehouse on February 5, 2018.

The campaign's emphasis on the need for people of different races and social and economic classes to come together to address a range of issues holistically was, however, very foreign to many of today's activists. Some of them hadn't been born when broad-based movement organizing was the norm. I heard them respond to the campaign's initiatives with mistrust and concern that their own special-interest organizations would be weakened or even co-opted if they joined in. Unite around the idea that such themes as poverty, racism, gun violence, ecological devastation, and health care are all connected? It seemed to be asking too much. The result was that people who should have been natural allies didn't sign on. In 1968 the issues had seemed simpler and less numerous.

The campaign's near total reliance on social media with a message that didn't lend itself to being conveyed in sound bites didn't help matters. Its themes and agenda are complex, and today's activists themselves have changed. Any one of the fundamental principles the campaign enunciated could have been a topic of hours of conversation and debate, but that doesn't happen in text messages and tweets.

In addition, the campaign had a surprisingly top-down approach, which is off-putting to those of us who believe in grassroots organizing and bottom-up organizational structures. We are not attracted to an organization that communicates through a series of directives, holds events prepackaged at the national level, and demands that local leaders not adjust their activities in any way that might better meet local needs or conditions.

These things were major obstacles to the Poor People's Campaign's organizing success in Vermont, but I was determined not to get hung up on them. I was excited about the ultimate possibility that the campaign would bring large numbers of activists together again to become a real force—an unsettling force—for change in many areas.

One of the things that most excited me was how the campaign intended to do this, starting with the very public and clearly stated intent to begin with a forty-day period of civil disobedience. The plan was to hold synchronized rallies at state capitol buildings across the country on every Monday afternoon from May 14 through June 21, then to immediately follow each rally with nonviolent direct action.

I was in! I had been playing it pretty safe for most of my adult life, and had never participated in civil disobedience to the point of being arrested. When I had demonstrated against the war in Vietnam as a student at the University of Wisconsin, I don't recall ever being at serious risk of arrest, despite a heavy police presence. In 1968 in Chicago I was in the Hilton Hotel recovering from my appendectomy, not out in Grant Park. Later, my legal career made arrest too consequential if I was going to continue helping other people with their immediate problems.

But for a decade, since the 2008 recession had unleashed such horrible consequences on so many at the hands of a few greedy bankers and housing lenders, and interracial tension had increased so markedly with the exposure of repeated murders of young black boys and men at the hands of so many local police departments, I was hard put to understand why more people weren't out in the streets demanding change. I was more than ready to join those who were.

I felt I had spent my entire adult life working hard to make life better for low-income working people and people in poverty: the mentally ill adults relegated to the Bronx State Hospital because community-based services were not available; the families I worked with as a social caseworker in Vermont; the people with disabilities for whom I tried to find jobs; my Legal Aid clients; the many disabled adults in desperate need of SSI but with no one to take their case; the overwhelmed mothers accused of neglecting their children; low-income women who desperately needed medically necessary abortions; and on and on and on. My work had resulted in the improvement of life for many, but somehow our society seemed inherently structured to make life harder and harder for poor people, despite the huge increase in the overall wealth of the country. Sometimes it felt like more than I could stand, and now, topped by the election of Donald Trump and the racist, misogynistic, oligarchical actions he was taking, I needed a way to express myself loudly!

So I found myself one evening in May in a church basement, taking a mandatory training in nonviolence, a requirement for participation in the direct actions. I'd had one other such training when I joined the legal team monitoring the border crossing of protesters on their way to the Summit of the Americas in Quebec City in 2001. This one seemed much the same, with the most important piece of information seeming to be the phone numbers that were handed out and the advice to write them in pen on our forearms so they couldn't be lost or confiscated. It was reassuring to hear that the campaign had two volunteer attorneys to assist us if there were arrests.

It all sounded good until we got to the discussion of exactly what would occur the next day. The theme of the first week's rally was "Somebody's Hurting Our People: Children, Women and People with Disabilities in Poverty." The plan itself was simple: After the rally those of us who were going to participate in the direct action would enter the crosswalk in front of the Statehouse and remain in the street blocking traffic. Our action, and whatever followed by way of police action, would bring attention to the campaign and its message by the publicity it would garner.

But then the trainers went on to say that to participate in the blocking of the street at 4 pm we each had to be present at 10 am for another preparatory session, no exceptions. I was completely deflated and found myself blinking back tears of frustration. I was ready and able to finally risk arrest for something I believed in, but someone I didn't know and who didn't know me was telling me that because I had an appointment in the morning that couldn't be postponed, I couldn't put my body on the line in this logistically straightforward protest in the afternoon. Who were these people?

I could hardly listen as one of the leaders began to list other roles people could play if they couldn't be at the morning meeting: keeper of things, meaning the personal items of those involved in the direct action; legal monitor; law enforcement liaison; buffer car driver. I perked up. It seemed that four people were needed to drive their cars up to either side of the crosswalk to serve as a buffer to protect the protesters from angry drivers who might be tempted to run them down. That seemed like something I could do and I quickly volunteered.

The next day's rally began on the Statehouse steps at 3:00 as scheduled, with a light but enthusiastic turnout. The speakers were excellent, giving fact-based speeches that made clear the degree of poverty being experienced in Vermont and in the nation as a whole. The line up of priests, ministers and rabbis from Vermont's faith organizations, who stood solidly behind them, was impressive and provided strong moral and ethical support.

At 3:35 those of us assigned to drive buffer cars left the rally to retrieve them and drove them into position facing the crosswalk at precisely 3:45. Our "moral witnesses," as the campaign's direct action participants were called, paraded into the crosswalk and stood there, singing and chanting with their large and beautiful banners and signs. The rest of the crowd, who didn't want to risk arrest, gathered on the sidewalks on both sides of the street, joining in the singing and chanting.

Pretty quickly we realized that no cars were lining up behind the buffer cars, nor could any oncoming cars be seen in either direction. It turned out that one of the coordinators had given the police a heads up about the protest as a courtesy, and they had decided to block off the entire section of the street where the demonstration was going to occur and re-route the traffic to avoid any chance of confrontation between drivers and demonstrators. Our buffer cars were superfluous, and our moral witnesses were left to occupy the crosswalk for 45 minutes in complete peace, after which we all dispersed without incident. The lack of confrontation confused everyone.

The theme of the second week was "Linking Racism and Poverty." Just a few weeks before, a number of issues related to this theme had come to a head in the Vermont Legislature, including hard evidence of systemic racism in state government, discriminatory policing at the local level, and targeted arrest and detention of Vermont's migrant farm workers by U.S. Immigration and Customs Enforcement agents. So I was excited to take part in the rally and the second direct action, which we were told at the morning meeting would consist of the moral witnesses leading the rest of the group into the Statehouse after the rally, where we would then stage a sit-in at closing time.

We took a break for lunch, regrouped, then carried all of our many banners and signs down to the Statehouse for the rally, after which we entered the building on schedule with the moral witnesses in the lead. The lobby was packed full with our people. Standing just inside the massive front doors we listened to personal stories of racism and poverty from those who chose to share them. However, the legislature had recently adjourned for the year and that part of the building was deserted, save for the sergeant at arms and her staff, and an occasional tourist or two. Who, I wondered, were we talking to, besides ourselves?

Promptly at 4:15 the sergeant at arms began to close the building for the day and everyone was told to leave, including our legal observers, who we had expected would be allowed to stay inside with us. That left fourteen of us sitting on the floor a little nervously, but we continued to sing and chant, feeling safety in our numbers.

Then the capitol police dramatically closed the shutters on the large lobby windows and pulled the heavy velvet curtains tightly shut over them. That was a little scary. It cut us off from our supporters at the windows outside, who could no longer see what was happening to us.

The sergeant at arms scowled at us. I had interacted with her during the legislative session and she had been very accommodating to the need of the organization I was representing for space to hold a press conference. I felt badly that I was causing her difficulty. I didn't see her as being responsible for the terrible state of the world.

The police left us sitting on the lobby floor singing, chanting, and talking among ourselves for three hours. They hoped, we surmised, that we would tire of being there and voluntarily leave. At 7 pm sharp, however, a phalanx of law enforcement officers arrived in the lobby. The capitol police chief introduced himself and the rest of them to us: three additional capitol police officers, the Montpelier police chief, a couple of state troopers, and a game warden! The capitol police chief read to us from the "Capitol Protocol on Protests": a formal first warning that we were in the building without permission after hours and were therefore subject to arrest. Pointing to each of the side exits he said we were free to leave at any time, and would have five minutes to do so before he returned to deliver the next notice. They all then disappeared in the direction from which they'd come.

As promised, the officers returned five minutes later to deliver the same message, except we were now warned that in another five minutes anyone still in the building *would* be placed under arrest. The chief asked if anyone intended to resist arrest and after we quickly checked in with each other we told him no. They left again, then returned five minutes later, whereupon the chief informed us that we were now all under arrest and would be processed individually in the committee rooms off the main hallway.

Our processing was very respectful and polite on both sides. The officers lined us up along the hallway wall and directed us to file one by one into one of the committee rooms set up for processing. We went in, gave our personal information, and received a citation to appear in court on June 28, five weeks from the date of our arrest. Some from our group were joking with the officers. I couldn't understand what they felt was funny or light about the situation, and took the whole thing very seriously myself.

When everyone had been processed, we were let out the side door together to rejoin our faithful supporters, who had remained on guard and burst into cheers at our reappearance. After a roll call to make sure everyone was out and accounted for, and a song, we dispersed. Hungry, thirsty, and very stiff from sitting on the floor so long, I walked to my car and drove home, wondering exactly what I had done that day that might have helped save the world.

Between my arrest and the following Monday, I spent a lot of time thinking about why I was engaging in this civil disobedience. What I had said in the previous week's morning meeting seemed a little lame to me: that I was there because I was retired and had the time to get arrested in order to represent other people whose jobs would be in jeopardy if they took the day off. But the real question was, why did I think that anyone should be there, why did I think that anyone should get arrested? What was it we hoped to accomplish? There had been some publicity about the first two rallies and our sit-in and arrests on the second Monday, but nothing at all in depth about the children, women, and people with disabilities in poverty, or the level of racism and poverty in Vermont and the rest of the U.S. that had led to the campaign's revival in the first place.

The more I thought about it, the more I came to feel that my reason for being part of the campaign, and for wanting to continue committing civil disobedience, was not to accomplish some*thing*, but was simply to express my feeling that as a person of conscience I couldn't be silent any more. If it took this level of resistance to make other people think about what life is like for those among us who struggle for survival on a daily basis, then so be it.

I thought of those who had set themselves on fire during the Vietnam war to draw attention to the horror of that war, and by some strange coincidence, between the Monday of my first arrest and the following Monday, I came across an article in the *New York Times* about David Buckel, a well-known activist attorney for gay rights who had become a volunteer compost facility coordinator in Brooklyn, and who had just set himself on fire that April, in a protest suicide about what was happening to the planet.[32]

I couldn't get Buckel out of my mind. Cooking dinner, or in the shower, or just driving here or there, I found myself talking out loud to the unknown judge I would appear before a month later, explaining my actions as a necessity if people were going to wake up to what was happening around them. I couldn't name the change that had occurred in my thinking yet, but I had crossed the line from activist to witness.

My participation in the Poor People's Campaign was not another organizing project or political activity; rather, it was an expression of the

---

[32] *New York Times*, May 28, 2018, A17.

personal values I lived by. I knew that these values went back a long way in my family, and much farther than that to an ancient and fundamental tenet of Judaism, "*tikun olam*"—the duty of every person to leave the world behind better than they found it. Success in this endeavor would not depend on how much press we got or on anyone else's response to me; success, for a witness, is standing up for one's principles without regard to the consequences.

This new realization made me appreciate even more the group of people I was getting to know through the campaign's days of action, who were turning out to be the most compatible group of people I'd met yet in Central Vermont. Modest and unassuming, clear about what they were doing and why, they ranged in age from their 20s to their 70s or perhaps older, and included clergy, farmers, college students, low-wage workers, people with disabilities, and retirees. Some were gay, some straight, some black, some white, some brown. It felt good, finally, to be working with such a diverse group again.

The third week was organized around the theme of "The War Economy: Militarism and the Proliferation of Gun Violence." After the rally things went pretty much the same as they had the week before. The capitol police, now aware that those of us sitting on the floor after the others had left were not going to leave, wasted no time going through the protest protocol with us and then processing us again in the committee rooms. This time there were only nine of us, five from the previous week and four new moral witnesses. I wondered why the number of moral witnesses was going down rather than up, and why no one from the campaign leadership was part of the group arrested this week. Did they know something that the rest of us didn't? Their absence was otherwise hard to explain.

The five of us who were being arrested for the second time were cited into court for later that week. Why was that, we wondered, when the previous week's citation had been for a month later? And what *was* a "flash cite?" And who was going to tell us what to do next? Where were those two attorneys we had been told we had? No answers were provided to these questions when we were released, nor in the next two days, and when we arrived at the Washington County Courthouse on Thursday morning we learned to our surprise that we had no attorneys to appear in court with us; one was not admitted to practice law in Vermont and the other no longer traveled. Nor had any strategy been received from the national campaign to guide our next moves.

To say we all felt betrayed is putting it mildly. I tried, as someone at least familiar with general court procedure, to explain what I could about the thick packets we each were handed comprising the state's attorney's case against us. But I was on shaky ground—I'd long since forgotten whatever I'd known about the details of criminal law.

Included in each packet was an offer to have our case referred to the Montpelier Community Justice Center (MCJC), which, if we successfully completed its program, would result in the sealing of our record and dismissal of our case. As a former CJC director I was happy that I could at least explain to the others what that program was likely to look like. I was sure at that point that all of us who were arrested at least once during the campaign would stand trial together, but wanted to do that on one charge rather than multiple charges, and was happy to have the CJC alternative as a way to dispose of this one, and others that might follow. One by one we each got up and pled not guilty to preserve the status quo and were released on our own recognizance, with a release condition that we not be in the Statehouse after hours again. Before leaving the courthouse I accepted the CJC referral.

I was unable to participate in the direct action the following Monday. A plan to occupy the Pavilion building where the governor's office is located got thwarted almost immediately. The group ended up spontaneously blocking traffic in an action in front of the building and more arrests were made.

When the fifth Monday came along, I found myself undecided as to whether or not I wanted to risk arrest again. On one hand, I knew I would be violating the condition of release I'd been given, since it prohibited me from being in the Statehouse after hours, and sitting in there was again the plan. On the other hand, I was hard-pressed to understand why, if I were willing to be repeatedly arrested for the crime of unlawful trespass by remaining in the Statehouse after hours, I wouldn't be willing to do the exact same thing again just because it was now called a condition of release.

It seemed possible that with each additional offense it became more likely that I might go to jail, and being jailed seemed almost a selling point to me. My thinking was that if the two of us who would be getting arrested for the third time actually went to jail, it would get more publicity for the campaign and its message, which was the goal of the direct actions. It had been clear to me for a long time that most Vermonters didn't have a clue about the fact that many of the people in their own communities were living on extremely limited incomes or in downright poverty, but hiding it pretty well. The week's theme was "Everybody's Got a Right to Live: Education, Jobs, Income, Housing," which pretty much said it all. By the time the meeting ended I had talked myself into joining the other moral witnesses again.

After the sit-in, the two of us third-timers and one second-timer were duly processed and given flash cites again to appear in court later that week. Not a hint of jail, just another appearance before the judge. On Thursday morning I checked in at the courthouse, was handed my packet by the clerk, and sat down to read it, expecting it to read much like the two I'd read before.

Wrong. While I may have considered the underlying offense and the condition of release to be equivalents, it was clear that the law did not. The penalty for violating the condition of release was double the penalty for the trespass: six months in prison and a $1,000 fine. I didn't consider myself seriously in danger of being jailed for six months, but clearly I was in some kind of jeopardy that I hadn't anticipated. Furthermore, although the state's attorney had again proposed the previous condition of release, the judge had ignored his proposal and was seeking an order that I not be allowed on the Statehouse grounds at all. For anything. Until the case was decided.

When I was arraigned three days later the judge made it abundantly clear that he was not at all happy with me for ignoring the condition of release he had previously imposed. He refused to refer this third unlawful trespass charge to the CJC, and ignored my verbal objection to the new condition of release. This was of considerable concern because I'd been told that cases going to trial were taking two years to resolve. I wasn't prepared to be banned from the Statehouse grounds for two years, as almost every important rally or demonstration in Vermont takes place there, and with Donald Trump in the presidency there were sure to be plenty; in fact, I was one of three organizers of a "No One is Above The Law" rally being coordinated nationally by MoveOn and organized locally by Indivisible Calais, set to take place when called for at the Statehouse.

Furthermore, my understanding of bail law was that conditions of release are to be imposed for only two purposes: to assure the safety of the public and to minimize any risk of flight by the defendant. I felt it was pretty obvious that I was neither a danger to the public nor a flight risk, but the judge refused to budge, and that made me angry. I didn't just feel he was being severe, I felt he had entered an unconstitutional order.

In the two weeks leading to my next court appearance, I occupied my time working on an appeal of my new condition of release. I was encouraged in this by a former Vermont defender general, who agreed that the condition was unconstitutional and was worried that it would set bad precedent. I sank my teeth into it and produced a motion and memorandum of law that argued the condition was an overly broad restraint on my freedom of assembly and my right to petition my government, and as such amounted to punishment without conviction of any crime. The state's attorney did not oppose my motion, continuing to ask only that I not be in the Statehouse after hours. The judge, clearly surprised by my motion and memo, reluctantly agreed to substitute the old condition for the new one.

I was free again to frequent the Statehouse grounds, but I had missed the sixth and final rally and direct action. The arrests that day had swelled our total number of arrestees to thirty-one individuals, arrested a total of forty times. We learned later that this was more arrests than there had been in the entire history of the Statehouse put together, but still the campaign's fundamental message received little publicity.

I felt badly about not having been at the last rally to get some closure on the first phase of the Poor People's Campaign. The way things were going with the lack of in depth reporting on the campaign's substantive issues and the apparent meaninglessness of our arrests, I thought I might need some inspiration to get through the rest of the legal proceedings, so I took the Vermont campaign's overnight bus down to Washington for the rally at the National Mall on June 23 that would mark the end of the forty days of action. That helped. As hoped, the speakers were an inspiration in their commitment and solidarity, and the march from the National Mall to the U.S. Capitol and back, impressive.

On June 26, two days before all thirty-one of us who had been arrested at least once were to appear in court for arraignment on our first arrests, we met to sort things out and come up with a defense strategy. To my surprise and dismay, when the Vermont coordinators were asked how other states were handling their arrests and what the national Poor People's Campaign advised, the answer was that we shouldn't waste our resources fighting the arrests but rather get the charges out of the way as fast as we could and get on with the important work of registering new voters.

I could hardly believe it! "What happened to getting the message out," I asked?

My question was met with a shrug. A few people still seemed inclined to go to trial, but the overwhelming majority were happy to have permission to take the CJC referrals or plead no contest, pay a fine, and be done with it.

The judicial conclusion to my own civil disobedience was anticlimactic. The two unlawful trespass charges referred to the Justice Center were eventually dismissed and the records sealed after two meetings with a sympathetic reparative board and the completion of three writing assignments, two interviews, and a meeting with the sergeant at arms and the capitol police chief. The third unlawful trespass charge—the one the judge had refused to send to the CJC after I violated his condition of release—was dismissed by the next judge who rotated into the court in September. I changed my plea on the condition of release violation to guilty, which resulted in a $50 fine and twenty hours of community service. The tightly controlled national plan of civil disobedience turned out to be largely inconsequential in Vermont, except for those of us who now have a criminal record.

*   *   *

I'm happy to say that my family was very supportive and proud of me throughout. Jim, true to form, never said anything for or against my civil disobedience, but kept the home fires burning and food on the table throughout the forty days of action and resulting court appearances. Both children strongly supported my decision to engage in civil disobedience and helped keep my spirits up with phone calls and emails.

At the end of August, when granddaughter Florence was born, Elizabeth asked me if I would speak at her *simchat bat*, her naming ceremony, to welcome her into the Resistance, by that time a major progressive movement throughout the U.S., fueled by the election and presidency of Donald Trump. By then I was into my 2018 midterm election work, canvassing in New York State, New Hampshire, and Maine, but was more than happy to take time out for the occasion. As civil rights activist Constance Curry said, "it is indeed the telling of the stories that is important—the passing on of the legacy. Perhaps lessons of hope and courage can make the future way a little brighter, a little clearer."[33]

And so, on the day that Florence turned three weeks old and her friends and family gathered in Brooklyn to officially name her, I told her of her paternal grandmother Maya's participation in *Machsom* Watch— the organization of Israeli women who oppose Israel's occupation of the West Bank and the denial of Palestinians' human rights, and monitor the border checkpoints to discourage and document instances of abuse and humiliation; of her paternal grandfather Clinton's championship and advocacy on behalf of the Bedouin in Israel; of Jim's work as head of a tri-county antipoverty agency; and of my own legal and political work on behalf of the poor, women, and other underrepresented people. And then I closed with the following:

> I very much hope that by the time you grow up you will be living in a country where all people are treated fairly and treated well, and where it can truly be said that justice is being

---

[33] Constance Curry, "Wild Geese to the Past," in *Deep In Our Hearts: Nine White Women in the Freedom Movement* (University of Georgia Press, 2000), 35.

done. Nothing would make me happier. But if that is not the case, and you find that to be the kind of person you want to be you have to devote yourself to fixing the problems you see, then I want you to know that all of us here will be right there with you in spirit if not in person, with pride and admiration for your work.

And so, Florence, welcome to the ranks of those who are determined not to rest until justice and equality are a reality for all. Welcome to the Resistance! It's good work, and you'll be glad you did it.

I am.

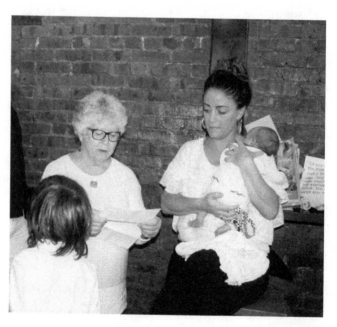

Welcoming granddaughter Florence (with mom) into the Resistance
Courtesy of Claudio Vasquez Photography

Clockwise, left to right: Grandchildren Edna (on dad's shoulders), Jack, Henry (with mom), Josephine.

About the Author

DINAH YESSNE is a native of St. Paul, Minnesota. She received her B.A. *magna cum laude* from the University of Minnesota in 1968, and her J.D. *cum laude* from Vermont Law School in 1981. A social worker, public administrator and attorney at various times, she has always been an activist, working for peace, equality and social justice all her life.

ACKNOWLEDGEMENTS

Like many memoirs, this one started out as an autobiography with an uncertain audience. That it's in your hands now, as a published work of literary value, is a testament to the strong support I have had from family, friends, and publishing professionals over the past two years.

Thanks to my earliest readers, Genie Grohman, Nancy Kleeman, and Sheila Reed, for their time, encouragement, and gentle but honest evaluations; to Rickey Gard Diamond, who critiqued the manuscript mercilessly, but knew I could take it, dig deeper, and produce a book with broad appeal. Thanks also to Amy Ehrlich and Sam Brown, my last readers, for their caring and support.

I also owe my thanks to my brother, Peter Yessne, and to my children Elizabeth and Daniel Keeney, for their fact-checking, reminders of forgotten material, and technical support; and to my daughter-in-law, Adrian Wade-Keeney, midwife to the cover design.

I must also thank the professional people who not only did their jobs well, but went beyond what they were hired to do and patiently answered my many questions: My editor, Michael Sherman; website designer Ben Witte; cover artist Sally Stetson; Gareth Bentall, my publishing manager; publicist Peter Bermudes; and the staff at Capitol Copy.

Finally, thanks to all of you who came forward at the end to help make this book a reality. Once again I am reminded of how often my life has been a group effort.